Converting the Crap!
How to Make your Real Estate Fortune Converting Internet Leads.

by Andy Herrington

Table Of Contents

Acknowledgements:

All of what I do is for my Family. Cara, Morgan, Samuel you are everything to me!

CHAPTER ONE
Introduction

"Nothing in the world can take the place of persistence. Talent will not; nothing is more common than unsuccessful men with talent. Genius will not; unrewarded genius is almost a proverb. Education will not; the world is full of educated derelicts. Persistence and determination alone are omnipotent. The slogan Press On! has solved and always will solve the problems of the human race."
— Calvin Coolidge

Over the years my success in the Real Estate World came from a surprising space, the Phone. Men are not supposed to like the phone, but frankly I always did. I was able to tackle the phone and make it work for me and the teams I was a part of. I started as most people do with cold calling. Grabbing the old phone book, starting at the A's and making my way forward. I had success, but definitely wanted a "better way". I put some ad's in the paper ... when I could afford it and again saw success. It was around this time that I joined a team. Seeing that my skill on the phone was not easily found, finding a team was not difficult. And now my phone work took on the entire day. 6 days a week 6 hours a day, for 6 years I was on the phone Honestly if I had been doing Cold calls that entire time, I'm not sure I'd be alive to be writing this book. But here I am, and here you are.

This book is based on one of the key ingredients to my success and the lessons shared here have come from the over 500,000 dials I personally made during my career as a Phone Specialist. About a month into my life as a Phone Specialist I began searching for a better way. There has to be some way to get people to raise their hands and tell me they are looking for, or at least considering a Real Estate move. My searches lead to print advertising, which was very costly, we improved it with 1-800#'s, Classified Advertising and Direct marketing, but the cost to produce leads was still very high. We needed to find a better, more cost effective way to produce leads. This led me to the Internet. SEO, PPC, and more. Branded webpages, squeeze pages and online classified ads. Frankly over the years I have done a bit of everything to produce leads (we will discuss the best of them in this book as well.)

We began to see great success in creating leads, they were coming in bunches and there was the abundance I was looking for. However, they were not converting, (at least not at first) I too said the same thing you probably are saying today. "INTERNET LEADS ARE CRAP!!!!" We could produce them at the drop of a hat (or well a coin) but appointments were hard to come by. It seemed like these internet leads just were not responding the same way all our previous leads responded.

Well, this book is going to chronicle how I created those leads, and the system I created to contact, convert and truly make a fortune from those "CRAPPY" leads. I will detail how to get your conversion percentage to be more the 3 times the average persons, just like I have for many others across North America. I will show you how I was able to produce almost 200 DEALS a year from internet leads time and time again. This book will show you how you too can become a huge success simply by "Converting the Crap!"

CHAPTER TWO
The Future Of Real Estate... The Internet!

Don't wish things were easier, Wish that you were Better! ~~ Jim Rohn

The Future of Real Estate Lead Generation has been the present for sometime now. Internet Leads. The internet is a marketing monolith that is very difficult to understand the full ins and outs of. Add to that its ever changing nature and you have what is obviously the most important new tool to hit Real Estate in eons.

Internet leads began permeating the marketplace in the late 90's early 2000's. They have come from many different sources and they have affected every industry in unimaginable ways. Almost every marketplace has been dramatically altered and those companies who refused to 'keep up' have vanished into thin air over the years. Right now the worlds largest Taxi company - Uber owns no cars, the worlds most popular media owner creates NO content (Facebook), The most valuable retailer (Alibaba) has NO inventory, the list goes on and on it is comes back to one reason for these companies ability to survive and thrive the internet.

Real Estate is no different. The big players in almost every area, at least in terms of transactions done all have the internet as a major tool in their business. However time and time again I hear about how INTERNET LEADS ARE CRAP. Over and over again, I am basically hearing people refusing to 'keep up' with what our consumer is obviously telling us is their new prefer method of obtaining information. So my first point in this book is simple - the internet is here to stay, you need to determine how you will use it to your advantage.

Next we need to understand that with this being a new medium for lead generation, we also need a new approach to converting these new leads. We cannot expect the level of results that other sources of business create from this new source either. We need to look at this new source and figure out its ins and outs, figure out its conversion percentages and more.

What we already know about the internet is that we can expect to have more control, lower costs per lead and earlier detection of the possible client than we have ever seen before. After years of dealing with internet leads and creating a system to contact, follow up with and convert these leads, I know that when we create internet leads and use a proper conversion style, the results can be amazing and frankly limitless.

Now there are numerous books you can buy and a huge number of companies you can hire to build and find Internet Leads for you, however, a core understanding of the leads generated by the internet is needed for the conversions systems that are discussed in this book. So to begin I am going to detail those understanding so we are all on the same page.

Unless you try to do something beyond what you have already mastered, you will never grow.
~~ Ronald Osborn

There are two types of Internet marketing that every successful company needs to do. One is Brand Building, and the other is Lead Creating. Let me say that again - You need to do BOTH in order to be a huge success.

Brand Building marketing is about creating an impression in the clients mind, and making the brand (YOU) associated with any and all thoughts about the service we offer. When speaking about the Internet three main sources of Brand Building marketing comes to mind. 1. Your Branded Website, 2. Search Engine Optimization, and 3. Social Media. With these items the main job and focus should be about creating mindshare for your brand with your clients. They should be about creating loyalty, and an understanding of what your brand is, what it stands for and how you are similar to your target clientele. A secondary function of generating leads is a huge advantage to have here as the leads created from this when done properly have a much higher conversion percentage.

Lead Creating marketing is solely about generating a name and contact information. The most important information you can gather is Phone Number, Name and Email Address, in that order. To many people believe that email address is enough, but this is simply not the case. In fact a good way to look at this is that a lead that is created with Email only is more of a Branded opportunity than a appointment opportunity. Yes I can convert some emails to an appointment but mostly I only am getting the opportunity to keep my name and brand at the top of their mind on a hope that it becomes an appointment.

When speaking about Lead Creating marketing online, we look at Low Brand Squeeze Webpages, Pay Per Click advertising, Local Search Engine advertising and Online Classified advertising. For these the main job and focus should be about creating LEADS! Names and Phone numbers for us to get in contact with. Emails are OK but frankly do not create massive increases in business. Phone numbers allow for a conversion to appointment percentage that email just cannot come close to. The best plan for all of these sites is a simple exchange formula, the Lead's contact information in exchange for other information that they find valuable, usually pretty pictures and prices.

It is much easier to double your business by doubling your conversion rate than by doubling your traffic. ~~ Jeff Eisenberg

The Sources of Internet Leads

Lets look at the main sources used in Real Estate to generate leads. Frankly there are really two things you need to worry about when generating internet leads, the first is Traffic, for most people that is the art of getting on the front page of the search engines. This allows you to drive many people to your site. Then the next step is Conversion, this is how well your website turns the traffic into a name and phone number. I will write about each of the different methods to accomplishing both of these key ingredients.

TRAFFIC
- ☐ Search Engine Optimization,
- ☐ Pay Per Click,
- ☐ Local Search Engine Traffic,
- ☐ Tag Marketing,

CONVERSION
- ☐ Branded Websites,
- ☐ Low Brand Squeeze Webpages,
- ☐ Online classifieds and
- ☐ Head Office Branded web leads.

TRAFFIC
Search Engine Optimization (SEO)

For me this is the Most expensive and difficult way to generate traffic. For the individual Realtor, it is a world where you are constantly playing catch up with all of those that started before you, and competing against bigger companies with much larger marketing budgets as well. The ever changing landscape of the "algorithm" that determines the ranking order for the different search engines make this form of traffic generation very difficult to master. If you happen to understand SEO yourself and can play with all of the different Meta Tags, Keywords and other backend mumbo jumbo that is involved with SEO, then go ahead and try, just don't spend so much time building that you don't have time to respond. For everyone else, I don't recommend attempting SEO as a viable option to generating traffic. i.e. Don't hire a company to do this. Also, SEO is only an available option for your personal Branded Webpage.

Pay Per Click (PPC)

This is the easiest and quickest way to generate traffic. It can be costly however you have a high level of control over the costs associated with it. While again you can do this yourself, and for the agent starting out, I would recommend that, once you can I would hire a company to do this for you. There are amazing tricks to getting more for your money that only those who are consistently active in the pay per click world seem to know about.

I mentioned the level of control, and that maybe one of the biggest draws to PPC. You can control 'where' your ads are shown, as in where the computer that is searching is physically located as well as the obvious which keywords they were searching for. You can control 'when' your ads are shown, Days of the week, hours of the day. You can control the budget, total and cost per click, and obviously you control the destination of where the clicker ends up. This is the highest level of marketing control available to the Real Estate Professional.

PPC can be used for both the branded or low branded squeeze pages (when done correctly).

Local Search Engine Traffic

This is an interesting and frankly ever increasingly important way to generate traffic. Also it is FREE. Yup free, no cost except time. With this you create a profile with the search engine for your company and obtain ratings and reviews from your own past clients. This also works with other Social Media platforms to create a list of possible connections for a local result when searching for any given search term. This is a system where you have very little control, but can effectively get on the front page for little to no cost whatsoever.

Local Search Engine traffic works only with your personal Branded Webpage.

Tag Marketing

This is a very interesting and cool marketing piece that makes it so people who have shown some interest in you and your service will have their computer 'Tagged'. This tag allows you to then appear as though you are advertising all over the internet, especially on some perceived big, expensive sites, such as YouTube. For a period of time, the lead will see your advertisement everywhere they go on the internet. It truly allows you to continue to market to the leads that got away in order to raise your conversion percentage.

In general it is low cost and fairly effective, it is a good addition to the other Traffic generators to raise your brand and try to bring back people who were once interested.

Tag Marketing is best used with a branded Website, but could potentially be used with a low brand Squeeze webpage as well.

CONVERSION
Branded Websites

This is your typical www.yourname.com website, with the picture of the agent, company name and logo right up front and centre. It should provide a source of high quality information about you, your company and real estate in general. The very best branded sites have full marketplace capabilities and information about numerous homes for sale. It should provide a level of Free information, however once the lead wishes a deeper level of information it should incorporate a branded Squeeze page to extract from the lead a name and phone number. These squeeze pages can also be attached to your branded Social media platforms to attempt to generate more leads like these. Not having this last part is the single biggest mistake most Real Estate People make.

It is a complex balancing act of where to extract the information. Provide too much free and you will get no names, provide nothing for free and you will get no names. Find the right mix and you will get names, phone numbers and email addresses from people who are willing to attach themselves to your brand. The leads found here are the highest quality leads on the internet. They are also the hardest to generate, conversion from visitor to lead on a normal Branded site is 2-5%.

Low Brand Squeeze Webpage

This is a Webpage that effectively has no brand awareness goals at all. Your name and brand will be located at the bottom of the page in the copyright section. The pages is about providing information the lead wants most in exchange for their contact information. It is a straight forward exchange and there is really very little sneak peak at the information. The reason it works here and not on a branded site is the "attachment to a brand". The lead is earlier in their buying process and are not willing to let a brand know their information but need the information to start making a decision on how to proceed. They hope that this low branded (unbranded in their eyes) site will give the information and they will not have to talk to a salesperson. Because of this these pages will convert at a much higher rate 12-18%. We get more names and numbers, but the people are less attached to our brand and harder to convert into face-to-face appointments (right away).

Online Classifieds

This is a free service that is fairly time consuming, but can produce quality leads. The leads generated can be direct response via Telephone, Email or they can be pushed through our branded or low branded squeeze pages. To make this work best I suggest using a generic Gmail or Hotmail email address. This will allow you to push the boundaries of what is allowed on the sites without risk of losing your key email address's ability to post on these sites. Posting of Homes is the most obvious and straightforward method, I recommend using your good email address for these. Also you should be constantly changing the call to action methods as this method attracts users who want to Phone, and Email. These ad's should be removed and run again every 24-72 hours or pay for the

Featured ad's. Then with the other account, post adds for your low branded squeeze page in the services section as well as the homes for sale section. Use as many online classified sites as are available as they are free, and copy and pasting the ad should not take too much time. Don't avoid a site because it is not used as much as another, just concentrate on the busier site more.

Head Office Branded Internet Leads

These are leads created by your corporate head office and distributed to the real estate salespeople. These leads are great, they are just a small step in quality below the branded website, and obviously we have no control over how many or when we might get them, however it is well worth the effort to ensure that you have completed and the steps that your corporate head office requires for you to be eligible. These leads are ready to be attached to a brand and usually are asking for an appointment. This is basically free since you are going to pay your fees either way. So be prepared to handle these leads when they come.

Social Media

You will notice I didn't say much about Social Media here, in general Social Media produces very, very little in terms of leads unless it includes a low brand squeeze page in it. It is a powerful branding tool, but not a lead generation machine.

Conclusion

With all of these options available to us, every realtor should be generating a level of internet leads, and then converting them into business. Each of us can create growth in their business solely by treating the leads we create with a bit more respect. Once we handle them in the proper manner, we will see the opportunity that lies in internet leads. Once we do, the opportunity is endless where we can go with it.

I failed three times because I had not taken the time to get all the facts. After that I learned my lesson well. ~~ Milton Hershey

The Myth of "The Quality of the Leads"

This is something that I hear from everyone I coach, meet or hear from via email or Facebook or Twitter. It is this worry about the Quality of the Leads they getting or generating. "Are they good enough?" "They are crap!" "There is nothing happening here"... I hear it all. And while there are differences in leads in regard to quality of the conversion percentages, the quality of leads are solely what YOU believe them to be. Let me write that again in big letters too, THE QUALITY OF THE LEADS ARE SOLELY WHAT YOU BELIEVE THEM TO BE!

We all know someone who is an impeccable cold caller, and is truly successful in picking up the phone, calling the phone book, booking appointments and making money. There is no doubt that in quality of conversion percentages that cold calling is the lowest end of the spectrum, however, the leads themselves are free and you have basically an infinite amount of leads, all you need is the ability to do the work and the time to do it and the results will come.

With that in mind, lets look at the spectrum in regard to average conversion percentages (from phone specialists not active full time salespeople) to APPOINTMENT from a bunch of different types of leads this is a conversion from lead to appointment over a period of 12 months.

Conversion Percentage
- Cold calling - 1%
- Farming – 2-3%
- Unbranded Internet Leads – 15% plus
- Unbranded Print Leads – 20% plus
- Branded Internet Leads (third party "i.e. Head office leads") – 30% plus
- Branded Internet Leads (first party "from your website") – 38% plus
- Branded Print Leads – 57% plus
- Referral Leads (business referral) – 75% plus
- Referral Leads (client referral) – 93% plus
- Repeat Leads - 97% plus

So with this in mind, if you have been doing a business based on repeat and referral leads for a long period of time and then add in Internet leads of any caliber and expect a similar conversion, you will become frustrated with "the quality" of the leads. However, you may be getting a good quality conversion and not even realize it. Each lead type needs to viewed in its own light not compared to other types of leads.

Remember how it was at the beginning of trying to build your repeat and referral business, it did not happen overnight. It takes years to build up that business and most new Real estate agents might get a couple repeat and referral leads in their first couple of years. The same build up occurs with any other type of lead you generate.

If you get 100 unbranded Internet leads today, having never dealt with them before, I would expect a conversion percentage (to appointment) of 6-8% over the year if you work the leads properly. Not the 15% you will get to over time as you become proficient at dealing with the leads and doing the follow up calls properly. You also might not see a single appointment for 3 or more months. This is because of where on the "Buyer Cycle" the Internet leads come from. With Internet lead generation we are now getting leads from phase 1 and 2, in the past those leads were much more rare. The lead is much more skeptical and skittish at this point and booking an appointment the first time we speak is a lot more difficult. These leads are more about follow up and providing that information and advice that we need to as an advisor. To get our conversion percentage up we need to become more understanding, less pushy and we need to have amazing follow up skills.

So you might be asking since there are obvious differences in the conversion percentage, how can I say that Lead Quality is a myth. Well Conversion percentage is only one factor in determining quality. Leads also need to be judged on their Coast Effectiveness, amount of supply and the time involved in converting them. Then when we put all of this together we can truly determine the quality of the lead. So lets look at the average cost per lead for those same types of leads.

Cost Effectiveness:
- Cold calling - FREE
- Farming – $50-120 (note: cost per appointment as lead itself is free, but ad campaign is costly)
- Unbranded Internet leads – $7-10

- Unbranded Print Leads – $15-20
- Branded Internet leads (third party) – $2-7 (sometimes FREE)
- Branded Internet leads (first party) – $15-30
- Branded Print Leads – $120-150
- Referral leads (business referral) – $50-200 (sometimes FREE)
- Referral Leads (client referral) – $200-400
- Repeat Leads - $200-400

Amount of Supply
- Cold calling – High supply
- Farming – Fixed supply (by choice)
- Unbranded Internet leads – High supply
- Unbranded Print Leads – High supply
- Branded Internet leads (third party) – Low Supply
- Branded Internet leads (first party) – Medium Supply
- Branded Print Leads – Medium Supply
- Referral leads (business referral) – Very Low Supply
- Referral Leads (client referral) – Low Supply
- Repeat Leads - Low Supply

Time needed
- Cold calling – Very High time
- Farming – High time
- Unbranded Internet leads – Medium time
- Unbranded Print Leads – Medium time
- Branded Internet leads (third party) – Medium Time
- Branded Internet leads (first party) – Medium Time
- Branded Print Leads – Medium Time
- Referral leads (business referral) – Low Time
- Referral Leads (client referral) – Low Time
- Repeat Leads - Low Time

Now some of these numbers may seem surprising, but this is the truth. The cost to create Repeat and Referral leads is High and the supply is low, but based on the low time needed plus the high return it is absolutely worth the cost. Farming when done really well is very expense per appointment but can have a very good return on investment over time. The lead itself is free and you can farm to as many as you want but once we make that choice the supply becomes fixed. The ad campaign to build the reputation is where the costs arise and the time needed to convert the leads especially early on in the process is often as high as cold calling.

So when we really look at conversion versus cost we will see that all leads are of similar quality. High supply leads cost less and take more time, where low supply leads cost more but take less time. It is simply a matter of the time I spend with those leads to convert them. The key for any business is to find what is seen as gold and then go to work to mine it.

We must to stop the discussion of the quality of the leads and instead determine do I have the time to convert them or not. If I am making a sufficient living from what I have, I don't need to add more leads or new types of leads. However, if I do need different types of leads, I need to look at cost vs. time and figure out what works best for my business. And evaluate those leads based on others like it, not a completely different category.

Lastly, say this to yourself: "If I am adding leads and not converting them, the problem is with me not the leads." This is the only truth about leads that really matters.

CHAPTER THREE

Understanding the Leads

Without a real understanding of who you are dealing with and what your ultimate goal is in your interaction with them, you are just a monkey throwing poop
~~~Andy Herrington

Understanding the Leads

I called this book "Converting the Crap" because I truly believe that the Real Estate Profession as a whole has grossly misdiagnosed Internet leads as CRAP. It is a huge misunderstanding that is frankly affecting our industry in a huge and negative way. You see the clients have made it very clear that they want and are going to use the internet to research and shop. In really all areas. Latest stats from NAR show over 90% of people starting their real estate transaction on the internet and that people take approx. 4-6 months to complete a transaction and another 2-4 months to close the transaction. This means that right now if your Real Estate board was going to sell 10000 next year, which isn't a big Real Estate Board figure, approximately 4500 people (90% of 1/2 a year sales) are online looking for information right now. Over and over again these people who are online are raising their hand and telling real estate people that they are interested in information. Sadly also over and over again we as an industry and writing them off as CRAP.

This is because there are also a whole bunch of people online who are looking but are unable or unwilling to by in the next 6 months. So one of the first jobs we need to do as an Internet lead converter is try to sift and sort the leads into possibles and not possibles. Possibles obviously deserve more of my time, but not possibles should not be ignored, for every single possible was at one time a not possible.

Internet leads are kind of like being a hitter in Baseball. If you focus on the sheer volume of 'not possibles' you are going to be disappointed time and time again. The stats from my own personal research shows that 66% of your opportunities with Internet leads comes from leads you have had for 9 months and spoken to more than 5 times. Also a quality conversion percentage to deal from leads over a period of 1 year is 6-9%. Talk to many people making money from internet leads and you will see a 2-3% conversion rate. This is because they have given up on the leads to early and are not doing proper follow up. But with these stats in mind, you can see why many people when focused on the conversion percentage would say "the leads are CRAP!". However, using that same logic we can say that Ty Cobb was a Crappy Hitter since he got out 63.4% of the time (For those unaware Ty Cobb has the greatest Batting average in the history of the sport). Don't focus on the negative, focus on the positive. The ROI on internet leads is the very best in Real Estate, don't let the low conversion percentage fool you.

This is about our mindset for the leads. It is most important because I believe wholeheartedly that whatever you think the leads are... they are. To further understand these leads lets look at the Buyer Cycle of the average home buyer and learn why these leads convert the way they do. Lets look at how the clientele that we find online behaves and shops so we are able to communicate better with them.

It is not the strongest of the species that survives, nor the most intelligent, but the one most responsive to change.
~~ Charles Darwin

The Buyer Cycle

To truly understand the leads that you are creating and what is the best way to convert them, we need to first understand the Buyer Cycle. The Buyer Cycle is a look at the Average time it takes a buyer to move from "Hey I wonder if we should make a move?" to "I have a firm offer on my next home!". This cycle does not include your Constant lookers, because they don't really have that first thought, they are just always looking. It also doesn't include people who choose not to buy, because obviously they do not have the end of the cycle. In order to create this average, it does however include all the people who think, look and buy anywhere from 1-2 days to 10-12 months. When all that is taken into account, what we learn is that in North America the average buyer cycle is approximately 14 weeks (3.5 months). During this cycle the buyer goes through 4 main phases,

- Phase one is "Locating and Reading Information,"
- Phase two is "Looking at Pictures of Houses,"
- Phase three is "Looking Inside Houses,"
- Phase four is "Buying a home."

Phase 1 takes about 2 weeks. During this phase the buyer searches (usually on the Internet) for information on how to buy and does a wide search for homes. They are mainly trying to find a supremely good deal, becoming comfortable with the idea that what they want may be out there while reading up on what the steps in the process are. They are not willing to raise their hand or call a real estate agent or company. They are not even sure they will buy at this point. They often fill out forms to get information sent to their email from a Lead Converting Squeeze Page, and will ignore branded webpages that ask for the same information. They are "Just Looking", they have not made a firm decision that they WILL buy, but are deciding if it is going to happen. The leads from this section are much more skittish and guarded with their information when talking to a professional. They are really only looking for INFORMATION, so this is the best way to garner favour with them.

Traditional Marketing garners no leads from this phase. On average they are 3-4 months away from a firm deal if they choose to make a move. They are not ready to be attached to a brand in their mind and may be unwilling to book an appointment unless they truly see a huge benefit for them. They need to feel that they are not being sold to and they need to feel comfortable and safe.

This phase also includes many people that determine that they will not be moving at all.

Phase 2 is 4-6 weeks in length. At this stage the lead has determined that they are likely going to be making a move. They are starting to look at homes and are more realistic on value and price. They will begin to determine what they can afford and what they will get for that money. They are open to having a professional help them but are less willing to actively find someone to be this person. They are spending most of their time looking at listing pictures from the places they found that make things easiest, online, in newspapers and magazines. They are becoming attached to the people they see in the ad's and the places where they find the information easiest. They are still a little afraid to contact a Real Estate person, in any manner outside of email. Unless they see a super deal they are happy just becoming aware of the marketplace.

Traditional marketing does not garner many leads here. Branded Internet leads and Lead Converting Squeeze Page Leads are gathered in this phase as well. On average they are still 2-3 months away from a firm transaction. They need someone who will provide help easily and is truly looking after their best interests. They are now beginning to talk to friends and family and hearing the horror stories and 'scary' pitfalls to the Real Estate Industry. They need to hear from someone who is interested in helping them make a quality decision and shows a very different personality than what they have been warned against by their "trusted advisors".

This phase also includes some people that determine that they will not be moving at all.

Phase 3 is 6-8 weeks in length. In this phase the Leads are willing to have and understand that they need a real estate agent as they progress through to buying their next home. They continue to look in newspapers, online and they head to Open Houses and talk to agents. They are now are actively calling Real Estate agents and are unofficially 'interviewing' them to see who they believe would be a good fit. They will sign Buyer agency once they choose an agent they believe will help them and protect them. They are always looking for someone who seems to go above and beyond, someone who will do more and who seems better than the rest. Some can only see a benefit from a 'listing agent' because they believe that agent will cut commission and possibly end up in getting the buyer a better deal. If they can see a different benefit many will gladly follow that path.

Traditional marketing and Branded Internet Leads capitalizes on this group. Lead Converting Squeeze pages will not create many leads if any at this phase. Our traditional lead handling techniques can and do work here, but if you are encountering a huge amount of Listing agent only calls, it tells you that you are viewed as the same or worse than everyone else and a new approach may be needed. If you are being contacted via the internet they have built some level of loyalty to you and view you as a trusted information source, if you can live up to that persona you will be able to convert these leads at a higher rate.

This phase also includes a few people that determine that they will not be moving at all.

Phase 4 is 1-2 weeks in length, buying a home, from offer to firm. They are past marketing and have chosen an agent, bought a home, and really only Lawyers and home inspectors are interested in leads from people at this point.

All leads fall somewhere in the buyer cycle. Even people looking to list their home for sale normally start their process in the buyer cycle, and the listing occurs in the final 8-10 weeks of the cycle (late phase 2 / early phase 3).

What needs to happen though is that we need treat people differently during each step of the process. We also need to understand that while this is an average cycle, many people take longer than 4 months. Our level of patience and ability to provide the level of service the client needs at each stage, will allow for us to convert more of our leads into deals, and frankly it will make it happen quicker as well. Pressure needs to be placed at the right time in the right amount. Once we become good at that we will see a huge increase in the results we see from the leads we create. The quote at the begin of this chapter really does say it all, become responsive to the changes your client goes through and be prepared to alter how you deal with each stage.

"Y" Deal with clients differently!

As a realtor in 2010 we need to understand exactly how the marketplace is changing. One of the most impressive changes is that "the Baby Boomers" are no longer the only generation driving the marketplace. While they are obviously a major factor in the market, they are being quickly bumped out of top spot by the emergence of Generation Y , along with it smaller counterpart Generation X. As a group they represent over 20% of the population, which for Canadians means approximately 6.7 million people and by 2012 Gen Y will encompass the entire 18-34 age bracket (Our First Time Home Buyers).

Now Gen X and Gen Y encompass' people born from 1960 through 1994. Gen x is a smaller group but they share very similar upbringing's and styles of behaviour. They are the mild mannered version of Gen Y. As a quick metaphor, Gen X is Canada, and Gen Y is the USA. The important part is that together they are a major force in the marketplace and they deal with salespeople and technology very differently from their predecessors.

Let's get to know this 'new Clientele' just a little more intimately. As realtors when we know how they think we can adjust ourselves and provide the level of service they look for and

About Gen X & Y:

- Are very independent – due to working mothers, divorce, day care, technology - ¼ is in single parent family, ¾ has a working mother, most of the time the child has been the Centre of Focus for the home!
- They Feel Empowered – They are owed something from the world, they are the "trophy generation"
- One of the most EDUCATED GENERATIONS of all time over 60% have completed a College diploma or University Degree
- Have always lived in a Disposable society – new iPods, video game machines, cars, clothes, cell phones, computers, printers.
- Money has little to no value as they have always spent and bought whatever they wanted. (Home values rising for 11 years in a row told them money is easy.)
- Have access to unprecedented information – on the internet, the amount of T.V. channels, a shopping mall on every corner, outlet malls, Online shopping, DVD's, Wikipedia,
- Not loyal, they are about making life easy and simple, whoever provides that is who they will use.

What does this mean?

1. Everything in their lives has lead to the belief … THE BELIEF that if I cannot get what I want here, I can get it there! So if they do not get what they want they will move on to the next source until they get it.
2. They prefer directness over subtlety – Give it to them straight. Will make decisions when logic is seen.

They will initially want based on emotion but will not buy without logic.
3. 86% have clicked on banner ads, and sponsored links --47% higher than older generations.
4. They do a lot of independent research when choosing what to buy.

How do we as realtors use this knowledge to provide better service?

Based on the unique characteristics of Gen Y, we defined need to take a new approach in order to attract them to us and to cause them to choose us as their realtors.

1. **USE their MEDIUMS**. Attract and communicate with the New Clientele using quick response techniques, consider enabling them to communicate and express themselves, using Email, web forms, social media and via Text Message. Remember, they are not loyalty based (Baby Boomers) they are ease of use based. Make things work for them in their lives and they will stay.

2. **Provide Immediate Value**. To overcome the new Clientele's need for information RIGHT NOW, provide them access to the best information as quickly as possible. Be available and reach able when they need you to be. This does not mean become their slave, but have many options for the client to reach you through.

3. **Use a Personalized Approach**. The New Clientele responds amazingly to experiences that allow them to personalize and customize their interactions. They have always been the centre of attention and had things done with their specific needs in mind, they are not interested in following your system, but in creating a system for themselves. Put them in charge or at least make them feel that way.

4. Take a Logical Approach. The New Clientele responds well to straight shooters and is used to making logical based buying decisions based on information and fact. They have been programmed through their upbringing to make decisions based on logic. Emotional attachment is first but solidified through logic.

Taking the time to identify our clients and their needs then selling to them they way they want to be sold to is the first step to becoming a successful Realtor. We cannot use the same techniques we have always used, not because they no longer work, but because the new client doesn't respond to them. When dealing with our Baby Boomers, what they have always wanted remains mostly intact, but as our clientele shifts, so too must our style of service.

CHAPTER FOUR
Systems for Lead Management

"Great customer experiences are those that espouse trust, convenience, relevance and intelligence". - Anthony Leaper

This is a sore spot for most Salespeople. Database's can physically drain the energy out of the creative, energetic salesperson. However, they are the greatest tool in allowing the Salesperson the ability to sell more and more homes. I will detail some examples of different CRM's but this is not a complete list by any means. The list of tools and programs available is ever changing.

A CRM - Customer Relationship Management software program is an invaluable tool. Only second to a telephone in terms of income generating abilities. They are truly a required element to having a successful and repeatable business. Options available are numerous and frankly I am asked on a regular basis which one I recommend. My answer is steadfast - "The one you will use!". With that said let me outline a few systems I have had contact with over the years.

Advantage Xi - Desktop software with one time fee, but can be shared remotely with a team. I do not know how long they have been around, and did not have a clue how incredibly well thought out it is. When I say it shows, what I mean is that NO ONE could have a product this complete, without the advantage of years of time to do it. It is quite obvious to me that this company listens to what its users are asking for, and they ACT on it. And they have been listening, and acting, for a very long time.

Agent Office - This was my favourite for years, and frankly the tool I used most during my life as a phone specialist but unfortunately they have not updated it in a long time. When the current owner, "Emphasys", bought it, they said they were going to re-write it and I was truly excited. Unfortunately they never did. They still sell it but provide no meaningful support, which is why I no longer recommend it. It really shouldn't be on the market that way. They replaced it with Agent Office Personal Edition which has no similarity at all to the original Agent Office. It is an Outlook add-on. I have heard nothing but negative feedback on it so I do not promote it either. I really hate to say it but my advice is stay away.

IXACT Contact™ - The primary focus of this product is that it be easy to learn and use, and not be crammed with a lot of things you won't use. You don't have to be computer savvy to build your business with IXACT Contact™. All the features are easy to learn and use. And, because it's web based, there is no software to install. It is a serviceable product for a basic set-up.

PropertyBase - Salesforce is the most known CRM in the world, but frankly it by itself requires far too much customization for Real Estate agents in my opinion. It needed someone to mould it into something that worked for us, out of the box, and that's what PropertyBase has done. It is built on the Force.com platform but has the screens, features, and flow that real estate agents need. And if that's still not good enough for you, it's virtually completely customizable. This thing will absolutely knock your socks off if you want power and flexibility. Only products based on Salesforce can boast this kind of customization. If you want to play with the big boys, get out of the sandbox.

Top Producer 8i - Take your Real Estate contact management online! Besides tracking your contacts and transactions, Top Producer offers many different tools to help you do more business, faster and more efficiently - The difference between 'Contact Management' & "CRM"! Top Pro is the most famous Real Estate CRM in the world. I personally have never been a fan as I feel it is very complex. I have found in the past that Top Pro was more interested in making the product look good than on making the product do what realtors need it to do. Just one man's opinion and remember the best CRM is the one you will use, nothing more.

Wise Agent - WiseAgent is clearly one of the top Real Estate CRMs in the industry. If you haven't seen it in a while, they did an interface "makeover" not too long ago that really makes all the difference. Besides always hearing very positive feedback on their tech support, one of the things I like most about it is their always expanding selection of partners with which they improve their product. Most recently they added Contactually, which joined others such as MailChimp, Rapportive, Docusign and many others. If you're looking at Top Producer, you also need to look at this one.

ZOHO.com - Zoho is the only one on this list that has a FREE application. Up to 5000 contacts and 3 users can use the zoho product for free. It is a great place to go if you don't have a CRM or don't have the budget for one. It is not real Estate Based, nor does it have fancy tools and things that some of the others will have. That said it is FREE and online.

Once you have picked a CRM, run with it. Take the time to do things right and in the same way over and over again. The cleaner and more precise your CRM is the easier it will be to find the information you are looking for. Also take some time to watch and involve yourself in the tutorials and videos online to help you learn about the product you have. They all can do some pretty amazing stuff that will in the end make you more money.

Simple things that a Realtor should do with their CRM:

1. Input all leads - I am a huge believe in if you have a valid name and phone number, you should have it in your CRM. It should be "tagged" with enough information that you could find each file in anyway you could imagine searching for it. I.E. Lead stage (buyer/seller/past client/lead/discarded/do not call) Lead source (I.e. web/ad call/open house) Who it belongs to, or groups it belongs to (I.e. Farm/newsletter/Team member/COI...).

2. Quarterly Clean up - frankly every Realtor I have ever coached is behind on their database work. Take some time once a quarter to go back and check on what was missed - Things will fall through the cracks, but consistent check-ups will prevent some of the loss associated with those cracks.

3. Plans - almost every CRM has plans you can attach to your leads. Take the time to build the plans and run them. Listing plans, after a deal plans, Past client plans, Buyer Plans. These systems can generate thousands of dollars a year!

4. Email / Newsletter campaigns - just as they sound use the CRM to send newsletters and email campaigns to your clients. Keeping you top of mind in your clients.

5. Calendar items - using the calendar is what takes a CRM over the top - reminding yourself to contact people when you should as well as keeping your day timer up to date, the calendar is of huge importance.

I wanted to live deep and suck out all the marrow of life, to live so sturdily and Spartan-like as to put to rout all that was not life, to cut a broad swath and shave close, to drive life into a corner, and reduce it to its lowest terms." ~~ Henry David Thoreau

Enhancing the leads before you put them in your database is a great way to increase your return on investment, especially with internet leads. As anyone who has spent any time creating or buying internet leads, you know that there is a certain percentage of the leads that are created that are "Scrap" leads. Scrap leads really have 1 extra letter to make the word more polite. Simply put they do not have a valid name and number. However often times they will have a vail name or valid email, with an invalid number. It is those leads that I want to "enhance" the most, but frankly we should be looking to enhance them all.

Enhancing the lead is simply verifying that the info is correct and finding more. I am going to discuss those leads without a phone number most. Those that are "good" of the bat can have all of the following tips done to them in an attempt to find secondary numbers and to confirm the info that was given in the first place.

So we have a lead, it comes in from:

Santa Claus
1234 FU Street
New York, NY
Billsmithson42@gmail.com
123-456-7890

Upto- $75,000
3bed 3bath, 200sq ft

Now I know that Santa Claus is a top investor, or at least it appears that way from the shear volume of inquiries he makes all across North America. I also know that FU street does not have a 1234, mostly because I know it doesn't exist. I also am going to ignore the criteria inputted because frankly that rarely bothers me, they lied about everything else, I doubt that was something they took a lot of time on either. Lastly I know I am not in the 123 area code so this is likely a false number. So all I have is an email that frankly seems legit. In fact these are very often legit because while they don't want us to know who they are... they do want the Real Estate information I have access to. I am going to take that email address and try to enhance the lead.

1. Go to the computer and open 2 internet windows
2. Copy the email address into your computer memory
3. Go to 1 window and open google.com or bing.com and paste the email address in the search bar. Press enter.
4. Go to 2nd window and open Facebook.com - Login to your Business Facebook Account. Paste email address in search bar on Facebook and press enter.

5. Go back to 1st window and read Google entry - specifically hoping for linkedin, kijiji, craigslist links. These may have phone numbers attached to the email address.

6. Go back to 2nd page and see if there is a Facebook account, open it, go to ABOUT ME, see if phone number is attached. Send friend request to Facebook profile, when accepted check About me again for phone number.

7. Run any address's and phone numbers through 411.com (411.ca) using regular and reverse lookup, as well as doing a internet searches of names, addresses and phone numbers can also verify or uncover new information.

The main point of this is to do it quickly. 30-60seconds a lead is all you need to take. Try to find better info then go on.

Lastly for those leads that we cannot find a phone number for but do have a valid email. Setting up an automated email drip campaign; as long as it takes very little of your time; is your only option left. Do not expect a huge turn around from this style of contacting leads. Without a phone number more than 99% of your leads will never contact you. Sending information that doesn't quite match what they are looking for is a good strategy to attempt to get them on the phone in order to "fix" the problem. However, it is more difficult to book an appointment with a "angry" lead.

Emails should be concise and to the point, they should just be a written copy of the scripts you will use on the phone and should ask for the clients information each time. This is an example of what I have sent in the past.

Note: The BOLD are important.

Subject: Thank you for your request! Action Required!

Thank you for your request for **(Homes for sale in the _____ area)**. We are getting the information prepared for you at this time. Please respond to this email to approve the sending of the information you requested! This information is going to include:

- - Criteria 1
- - Criteria 2
- - Criteria 3
- Plus I include a Free report on Home buying that will help you save money and time while purchasing your next home.-{Note: Get one from about.com that you like}

I know this information will help you as you look toward purchasing your next home.

The information you requested is a bulk list of homes for sale in (Area Name), however, many of our clients have found that a more detailed approach is needed. **This improved list** includes more up to date and specific information of the homes for sale in (Area Name), including additional information such as property taxes, room sizes and additional photos. Also our premium list **includes Bank Sales, Power of Sales, Estate Sales and Other 'Distress' properties** that represent the best value on the market today. This additional information is **provided to our clients Free of Charge upon request**. In order to get the premium information simply (Visit www.yourleadgenerationsite.com/Freeinfo to get your free information) fill out the form below, reply to this email and a report will be generated.

Name:
Address:
City:
Province:
Phone Number:
Fax Number:
Email Address:

City looking to move if different from above:

Hoping to move in next 6 months (Yes or No)?

Do you want access to the Premium information, including room sizes and additional photos? (Yes or No)

Do you want info on Bank Sales, Estate Sales, power of sales and anything else that represents the best Value on the market today? (Yes or No)

Thank you

CHAPTER FIVE

The Psychology of Internet Lead Conversion

I don't know the Key to Success, but the Key to Failure is trying to please everybody! ~~ Bill Cosby

With internet leads comes a brand new problem to the Real Estate professional, ABUNDANCE! Abundance is readily available to anyone who wants it. This amazing steady stream of leads coming from a source that seems endless and is frankly overwhelming. It is both a blessing and a curse. Too many leads can be just as detrimental to a business as not enough. Because of the relative ease in creating the lead and low cost associated with it, many Realtors will end up with far too many leads, and without a proper system to handle the leads they will all end up in the garbage bin. The true key to finding success in internet leads is finding the balance between the number you create and the number you can handle "properly".

What does handling the lead properly look like? Well I'm going to go through 2 systems I have implemented to a high level of success in many different Real Estate Business across North America. One is for the Solo Real

Estate Salesperson, and One for the highly desired and effective Inside Sales Team.

Step one:

The most important part of the system is GETTING AHOLD OF THE LEAD. Physically speaking to the lead. That is what this system is based around. The more people we talk to the more appointments we will find.

Solo Agent Lead System:

Personally I think this is the perfect system for Active Agents:

1. First 3 days 2 attempts a day - 1 v/m on first call
2. Next 4 days 1 attempt a day
3. Next 7 days - minimum 4 attempts total - 1 v/m on last call
4. Next 14 days 0 attempts
5. Next 14 days minimum 7 attempts Total - Decide "do I give up?"

Total of 21 dials

This would be an acceptable standard to hold for yourself or any Active Sales Reps on a Team. Assuming that most people will accomplish approximately 70% of this most of the time (14 dials). That would be anywhere from 8-12 more dials than the normal Realtor®, and truly set up a much more intense approach to contacting and attempting to cultivate business from internet leads.

Inside Sales Team Lead System:

For an Inside sales team, my lead system expectation obviously grow. The Inside Sales teams sole purpose is to talk to and book appointments with the leads they are provided. They spend all day on the phone and therefore I expect far more from them. Their system looks like this:

LEAD WITH PHONE NUMBER:

1. First 7 days - 3 attempts per day - 1st call leave V/M - Hi its {name} call me back at {cell Number}
2. Next 7 days - 1 attempt a day - V/M on day 14 - Hi It's {name} from {company} I am calling regarding ... Call me back at {office#}
3. Next 14 days No attempts
4. Next 14 Days 1 attempt per day. - return lead to team leader if you are giving up.

Total of 42 dials

Step Two:
The rest of the system is the same no matter who talks to the lead.

1. Follow Script
      1. Intro
      2. Qualifying Questions
      3. Make an Offer
      4. Handle Objections
      5. Book appointment or Book Follow up

I have included scripts in this book that you can use. They are designed specifically with talking to Internet Leads in mind. They take into account all the different lessons you have read about and will read about in this book. They have been used in well over 1 million Internet Sales leads calls and have proven themselves to convert at a very effective rate.

2. FOLLOW UP

Statistics show that 66% your opportunity for business with internet leads lies when you have had the lead for 9 months and spoken to it more than 5 time. So a quality follow up program is imperative to the process. This means we cannot create so many New leads that we cannot provide service to the old leads. If we do, we will be throwing good money after bad over and over again. Each time the lead shows up as a follow up on our system we should be following the STEP ONE's system starting at #2 in order to get ahold of them again. For more info on this topic read the chapter - "The Importance of Follow Up."

How to Pick-up the Phone... and Actually Dial It

I know this sounds like a silly topic, how to pick up the phone. But you'd be amazed at how difficult a task this really is. If it was a simple case of grab the receiver in your dominant hand and lift, Real estate would be a much easier game than it is. The picking up of the phone is the easy part; the dialing is where the problems begin. So many Realtors, on a daily basis do their very best impression of a 15 year old nerd calling the head cheerleader. A lot of phones worldwide are stared at all day long, with nothing accomplished.

Dialing the phone is a MENTAL game. You need a good energy level, a positive attitude and confidence in yourself, your message and your ability to handle all situations that might come up. When you have achieved this you will see an amazing thing start to happen. Your ability to pick up the phone and dial will grow. Soon your love of picking up the phone will grow and then it will no longer be a task or a necessary evil, it will be an amazing part of your business and one you look forward to everyday.

51

Some things to try to help you build your Mental Game:

1. Set a reasonable daily goal for Dials, Contacts and Appointments. And a prize for attaining them.

2. Do not worry about everything on your day timer, only the stuff you can get to – YOU WILL NOT GET TO IT ALL! This is OK.

3. Use a headset when dialing, Stand and walk around when dialing, have music in the background (quiet)

4. Role play "out loud" a couple of successful calls prior to picking up the phone.

5. Take a break every 90-120 min for 5-10 min or if a client angers you on a call. Get up walk around take your mind away from calling. When you return refocus and begin dialing again.

6. Know that the hardest Dial is the first one. Call a friendly, or simply use the will power to begin dialing.

7. Watch funny or inspiring videos on youtube.com on your breaks.

8. Affirmations done "out loud" prior to calling or even prior to each call can work wonders. (try – "Helping people", "High Energy, Great Message, Lots of Appointments", "Here is my next appointment" or "I'm an Appointment Booking Machine")

9. Have a mirror in front of you and make sure you are smiling all the time.

10. Have a tally board so your accomplishments are noted and shown to the world. Know what is happening Daily, Monthly and Yearly.

Also read one of the earlier posts on Inspiration versus Motivation. This I hope will help a bit as you begin to get more in the habit of dialing the phone more and more every day.

Lastly, have you completed your own PERSONAL Goals this year? And what goal specifically can be achieved through you making these calls. What is the direct benefit to you to pick up the phone and dial? When you can answer that, you will be well on your way.

Email, instant messaging, and cell phones give us fabulous communication ability, but because we live and work in our own little worlds, that communication is totally disorganized.
~~~ **Marilyn vos Savant**

Alright so you have gotten a lot of leads from the internet and are finding them very difficult to get a hold of. Maybe we should send a bunch of emails, or leave voicemails as well. It seems like a good thing to do, I know the email is correct 95% of the time because that is how they expect to get the information they requested. Plus if I leave a voicemail and they don't call back that tells me something about their motivation doesn't it?

VOICEMAIL:

Well Let me say NO! It doesn't tell you anything about their motivation. Not at all. The fact that they are looking online at information and willing to fill out forms tells you more about their motivation than anything else. Leaving Voicemails tells me more about the agents motivation than the clients. You see, it is our job to get ahold of the lead and provide them quality service. It is not the Leads job to call us back. In fact that last line is so important I have hung it on the wall in every Real Estate Office I have been a part of. It should become a mantra of yours. It is not the Leads job to call you back. So with this new bit of knowledge lets look at what leaving a voicemail actually is to our business.

1. Time Waster - Well number one leaving a voicemail takes between 30-60 seconds, and I know that as a general rule you get far less than a 1% call back rate. During that same amount of time I could make 1-2 more dials, doubling or tripling my chances to actually talk to someone. So leaving Voicemail actually dramatically harms my ability to make money.

2. Handcuffs - Next is the fact that once I leave a voicemail it severely handcuffs my ability to dial the phone again. We have the feeling that we are bothering them, or may seem desperate. So we don't call them again and they end up talking to someone else and dealing with someone else. All because I left a voicemail that I knew would rarely cause them to call me back.

3. False sense of accomplishment - Leaving a voicemail puts the pressure on someone else, "the ball is in their court" and allows us to feel like we did something. Even when we know they likely won't call us back. We say well they must not be interested or if they really wanted me they can call back. We can write the lead off as "finished" in our mind rather than "active".

So does this mean we should never leave voicemail? NO! It doesn't, but it is a tool to be used sparingly and with knowledge about true expectations of the outcome from leaving the voicemail.

1. Voicemail should be left on a first call back from a direct contact from the lead. So they know you have responded to their request. This will most likely be a sign or ad call. Your message should be "Hi this is NAME from COMPANY calling in response to your Request for INFORMATION. Please call me back at PHONE NUMBER, If I don't hear from you I will try you again in about (15-60) minutes time. Thanks for calling COMPANY." This allows, heck even forces you to cal them again, since you told the lead you would. Future calls would not include voicemail.

2. Voicemail Should be left at the end of the first day of calling on an indirect lead (internet lead). This voicemail is simply left to see if they might respond. The voicemail is simple and to the point. "Hi It's FIRST NAME, Call Me back at CELL PHONE" That is it, no company name, no this is why I am calling, this message should have the same feel as though you are leaving this message for your best friend, however your phone is dead and they need to know a new number to call back to. The whole purpose of this is there are people who might call you back and for 1 voicemail, I am willing to spend the (now 5) seconds to leave this message.

3. Voicemail should be left when you are giving up on a lead either for good or for a period of time (I.e. 2 weeks or a month). This message should be tailored to the lead and should make them feel compelled to call in. Elude to great information that you have and want to get to them if only they would call you back. The end of the buyer offer works well for this if you do not have something specific for this lead.

EMAIL:

Email is simply Voicemail on Steroids when it comes to Real Estate. If voicemail is a time waster, Email can be a Time Destroyer. If voicemail gives you a false sense of accomplishment, Email is 100 times worse. Email is the preferred method for most internet leads for one sole purpose, They can ignore you! It is so they don't have to build rapport or have a relationship. They can use you and leave you. This there fore means that using Email to communicate with LEADS (these rules don't apply the same to clients) is a very poor way to create appointments and future business.

When all we have is an email you have two options and honestly I am OK with either option as a viable solution.

1. Is a Completely automated, build it once, set it and forget it Email drip campaign. This can be 3 emails to 33 emails, The longer it is the better chance one of these emails ends up working with you in the future. They should be sent every 2 weeks, they should be full of helpful information and a direct call to action. You can get tons of Free information to share from About.com, and the call to action should be a variation of the Buyer offer or the Seller offer, a link to your Lead creating website or anything you would put in a print ad as well. The real key is you should take as little time to set it up as possible. Then make sure that in order to put a lead into the follow up it takes less than 30 seconds to put them in the campaign. If that is the sheer volume of time spent on emails, then the return on investment for you will be worthwhile. Anything more is frankly a waste.

2. Ignore all leads that do not have a valid phone number (obviously after the Enhancing the leads stage has been completed). Just focus all your time and energy on people

with phone numbers, Call them, talk to them build rapport and book appointments. The more time spent calling phone numbers the more money you will make at the end of the year.

What you really need to do is focus on the dials, focus on the leads with phone numbers and focus on actually getting ahold of those leads. Talking to people is what creates business. Creating names and phone numbers is nothing compared to actually speaking with people. Sending Email is not the same, you are not a real person to them you are a virtual entity, and people have no loyalty towards a virtual entity. The best way you can look at it is that EMAIL is a Lead Creating Activity, not an appointment creating activity. And you only have so much time in the day to spend on Creating Leads. The majority needs to be spent on converting them.

Scripting is only as good as the speakers belief in the message, who wrote the words you use doesn't matter as much as do you believe in what they say. ~~~Andy Herrington

I include this chapter in almost all of my books because it is worth reading over and over again. It is such a key to having success on the phones that I cannot leave it out simply because some of you may have seen it before.

Scripting seems to be an evil word in many circles, but I know that whether or not you realize it, you are using a script each and every time you are on the phone. Over the days, weeks, months and years you have learnt what works and what doesn't and have formed some version of a script. What is really in debate is the extent of the script, how exact you are each and every time and who wrote the script. Personally, I have used other people's scripts and have written my own. The results have varied and not in the way many people would like to believe. Neither the 'do you own thing' nor the 'My script is the only right script' people will be happy when I say that I have had equal success from both version and equal failures from both versions.

What I have found is that there are five truisms to scripting no matter what you do, or where you are and I'd like to share them with you.

A script written down is far better than one in your head.
Once you write something down, you can set about a. learning it word for word and b. improving it over time. The first step in any scripting process must be to write it out in full. I am amazed at how many people fight scripting however they possess great scripting, they just have failed to write it out, and because of this their skills diminish over time and they have no way to check back and figure out what they are doing differently.

Belief in the message is the single biggest key in the success of any script
Ever wonder why some scripts work and others don't. Or how one person has amazing success saying something but it just doesn't work for you? Well it all comes down to believing in what you say. Belief in the Message; it is so important that it is my Tagline on my blog. People want to listen to someone who speaks with passion and sincerity, not a automaton that can easily spit out the "right words". So no matter how good the script is, if you do not believe 100% in the words on the page, the meaning behind them and that they are in the very best interests of the client, the success rate you will have will be miniscule.

"Short scripts require word precision, long scripts require message precision."
A short script such as a telephone script require word for word accuracy, where as longer presentational style scripts

need to allow the flexibility for message to message accountability.

WORD FOR WORD is needed for these short scripts as even the smallest change can have a huge impact on the results of the script. In fact, small words have greater importance than you given them credit for. In most instances the changes from original script to "personal version" involves what the salesperson sees as unimportant changes. They remove "insignificant words" or change them to a "similar" word. As a scriptwriter let me say that the words the salesperson think are important usually are not, and the ones they change are the psychological keys to the success of the script. For example picture a script with the following phrase – "It will update you..." and someone changes that to say "I will send ..." these are seemingly harmless changes, but psychologically speaking the message is drastically different. "I vs. It" – One instance is referring to an automated process versus one where the person will perform a duty. For many clients they are afraid to inconvenience someone else and will say no to an offer with I and yes to an offer with It. "Send versus update" – Send can be interpreted as the whole list each time, rather than update which will convey only changes to the list this can get a client to see a dramatic difference in the offer from what they can get themselves. Lastly, removing the word "you". This is the most common and surprising thing I see in "personalized scripts." You and any version of that word is the most important word in any script. The more you can say it without becoming a crazy person the better. Less 'I's' and more 'you's' is a great thing. It lets your client know that you worry about them and their needs far more often than you do for yourself and your needs.

Tracking is 100% necessary in order to improve a script.

Phone Scripts need to be memorized, internalized, and used for a period time where the results are tracked before looking for ways to improve and change them. Learning the scripts to a point where you can self evaluate if you are using them WORD FOR WORD each and every time you are on the phone, only then can we determine what the exact results are for a script. Then we can make MINOR changes one by one over time and see if there are repercussions or improvements. Most script changes result in a worse performance, certainly in the short term since the belief in the new script has not solidified in us yet. Tracking new scripts takes time and patience and too many people make sweeping changes or make changes too often to get a good handle on the exact results. Most script changes should be tracked weekly for a minimum of one month before any level of evaluation on its success or failure can be determined. Also you should only track one script change at a time. You can see just how long and involved it can be to implement fresh changes to a scripting platform. This is one reason why many people find a script and just stick with it, until it doesn't work anymore.

All scripts need to have a Customer Driven Approach or they will not work!

This is one that we hear over and over, but I am amazed how rarely it is actually utilized. "W.I.F.M. (Whats in it for me) is the radio station everyone listens to" is practically a mantra of every sales trainer I have ever spoken to... which is a large number by the way. However time and time again I see huge AGENT FIRST scripting mistakes. Right now the largest one I see is asking the lead if they have an agent helping them too soon in the conversation. Far too many people do this right off the bat, as the first or second question they ask. This question has no benefit to the client and has nothing to do with their purchasing or selling a home. Yes most boards require the agent to ask this ... before offering to provide services, but not before we find out some information about the lead.

This is one example, but the problem is rampant. When you have a script written out, examine it and put yourself in the mind of different buyers and ask yourself, could this question offend me, is this the very best way to ask this, do I feel like the agent cares about me or themselves? Do I feel extra or unwanted pressure from this question?

Scripts are our first impression with people most of the time, make them feel like we care about them first and ourself second and they will want to have more to do with us.

These five truisms have very little to do with the actual words that are said. I have personally used at least four different "other's Scripts" and 1 of my own that I have altered many times. My script was built from the best parts of other scripts and my own testing and improvements over the years, they have worked for people I have trained and for me over the years. However I saw many other people try to do this exact same script with little to no success. It all came down to understanding and respecting the truisms.

Your philosophy determines whether you will go for the disciplines or continue the errors.
    ~~~Jim Rohn

When building a script and spending time on the phones, you will begin to see that one of the most important tools you can have and use is an understanding of the philosophy of converting a lead to an appointment. This is an understanding of how to get people to agreed to meet with a sales representative even thought they likely would prefer not to.

The first step in the philosophy is to stop seeing yourself as a Salesperson. Instead view yourself as an ADVISOR. Someone whose job it is to advise the client of the marketplace and how to go about accomplishing their goal of homeownership. This is an important mental shift and can be used on the phone and in presentations. This is a key shift that will position yourself to earn more money and have less stress in your life. Advisors do not take ownership of prices or negotiations, they do not make promises, Advisors make observations, share information and provide advice so the client can make a quality decision, but whatever the client decides it is their own decision.

Once we have made that key shift in our minds, we can look at some of the philosophical tools we can use to our and the clients advantage.
1. Philosophy of Counteraction
2. Philosophy of Why
3. Philosophy of Consistency
4. Philosophy of Social Proof
5. Philosophy of Reduced Effectiveness
6. Philosophy of Previous Dealings
7. Philosophy of If

Lets review each of these and how we can use them to our advantage.

Philosophy of Counteraction

As Newton's 3rd law states - For every action there is an equal and opposite reaction. For sales, this is an understanding that our actions will result in counteractions from the client. In fact even a perceived action will create a counteraction from your client. According to Dr. Robert Cialdini, one of the most widespread and basic norms of human culture is counteraction. His rule is that if someone does some action for you, you will want to do a counteraction in return. This is commonly known as "you scratch my back I'll scratch your back".This sense of obligation ensures that relationships grow, and that transactions and exchanges that are valuable occur.

A favourite and profitable use of counteraction is to provide the action before asking for anything in return. You can see this being used by charities when they include the gift of address labels in hope that you will donate to the charity in the future.Although the "gift" is relatively inexpensive it plays upon our inherent need to reciprocate even when the gift was not asked for or even not wanted at all.

There are many ways that you can use this concept as a phone specialist. At the beginning of a call let the lead know you have done something for them, in return they will likely answer some questions. When Reminding a client of an appointment let them know you have done the prep work for them, they will be less likely to cancel an appointment.

Philosophy of Why

This is an understanding that people do not respond well to being told they "need to do something" without knowing WHY. As a phone specialist our job is to convince the lead to meet with a sales representative and they do not immediately want to do this. We need to explain WHY it is important to them to meet with us.

The Why is how to inspire people to action, but too often salespeople explain the features of a product or service which is explaining what a client gets, not why they should get it. Advisors inform a client of the benefits the client will get from following a specific action; this is why the client should act.

Philosophy of Consistency

People like to be consistent, so if they say yes, they want to continue saying yes. If they say no they want to continue to say no. A consistent approach is always useful. Small yes's can become a big yes. Now this doesn't specifically mean only the word yes. If they agreed with you that what you are saying is good, or right than when you ask for something they would usually not see as a positive, it will seem more reasonable. For the phone specialist, asking the right questions and making the right offers, then following with asking for an appointment creates a better opportunity to book an appointment that the client is a little afraid of.

Philosophy of Social Proof

People do not like to be the first person to use your service. They want to know that it is somewhat exclusive and they are better than others if they do use it, but having testimonials and a history of success will help you. Sometimes for the phone specialist this is a bit harder to incorporate, but reminding a lead "because of the sheer volume of business we do..." can remind them that there is a history behind your service.

In todays world much of this Social Proof needs to be found on the internet, in the form of social media. Many times your client will not ask you, or give you the opportunity to provide social proof they will have gone in search of it first. As a pone specialist directing them to places to find the social proof is a good way to end a call in all circumstances.

Philosophy of Reduced Effectiveness

This is the understanding that even when we do a great job of inspiring our leads to action, we will soon hang up the phone and our energy and positive words will slowly dissipate. They will talk to other people and those people will likely be less than positive about the action the client has decided to do. Also the human brain will get involved and begin going through all the scenarios including things that are highly unlikely and highly unsatisfactory or even scary. This means the client becomes less and less interested in performing the action they agreed to do. The next time you speak with them be prepared to revitalize their interest and do not be surprised or get frustrated that this is lack of inspiration is occurring. For phone specialists, I recommend speaking to a lead again to remind the lead about the importance, excitement and of course the benefits of the appointment any time that the meeting is more than 1 sleep away from when you originally booked the appointment.

Philosophy of Previous Dealings

People will judge future dealings with those that have happened in the past. This is truly important for the phone specialist. Know that our call is influence by all previous calls the lead has had from any salesperson in the past. This includes other "telemarketers" and other Real Estate people. You need to set yourself apart and understand that the client will not immediately be open and loving toward you. So do not expect them to be your friend, do not attempt to 'create rapport' on the first call, be business like and make sure the client understands you do not wish to waste their time, but are there to help advise them in regard to their upcoming real estate transaction. Also important is to leave them with a good overall impression of you and your company should you not get an appointment, as this will affect your future dealings with the client. Remember that sadly this good impression is counteracted by the many bad impressions that other telemarketers and real estate people are going to make before you talk again.

Philosophy of If

'If' is a very important and powerful word for the phone specialist. One of the worst habits we can have on the phone is attempting to pin down a lead on exact time frame or exactly where the client wants to go to early in the process. People are afraid of absolutes because they may not be right (goes back to the philosophy of consistency). However, taking away the absoluteness of the situation with a simply little "IF" can create all the difference. Use questions like the following to determine timing and location.

- If you did move where would you go?

- If you did move when would you do it?
- If everything worked out perfectly when would it happen?

When used correctly and consistently you will see a steady increase in the number of appointments, the number of attended appointments, the number of contracts and the number of deals. These philosophies are impressive tools that can vault any salesperson into the realm of the TRUSTED ADVISOR. And believe me, Trusted Advisors get more referrals and make a whole lot more money at the end of the day.

CHAPTER SIX

The 14 Steps to Lead Conversion

If you see the gold in the mountain, you will work hard and take the time needed to mine it out, if you see the rock, you will say it is a waste of your time. ~~~ Andy Herrington

1. Create Lead

We have already covered this in terms of internet leads, but obviously there are numerous ways to create leads and this 14 steps to lead conversion will work with all of the leads you create in your Business. Most people work best with just slightly to few leads to feel comfortable. This allows you to really work the leads to their maximum and frankly earn more money then having just right, a few too many or too many leads. It may seem a bit off but it is absolutely true.

2. Enhance Lead

Enhancing your internet leads is a step too many organizations skip. It should not take very long per lead, but the return on that time can be huge. The key to lead generation is having a phone number. So the entire point of enhancing a lead is attempting to find a valid phone number. There are a few ways to do this.

411.ca / 411.com are two website which allow you to use names and addresses should you have that information in order to locate a phone number. You can also use these sites if you have a phone number, to find an address and see if any other phone numbers are attached to that address.

Google.com / Yahoo.com / Bing.com - Any search engine is a good place to search names as well as email addresses. Email addresses can often lead you to craigslist / kijiji ads that the lead has posted in the past and could lead you to a phone number. The best part here is those phone numbers are usually cell phone numbers which are the best to have. Search engines can also lead you to social media sites which may have public profiles with possible phone number or job information.

Facebook.com - any social media can be helpful, but Facebook is the best. Take the email address and search Facebook for a user profile. See if the public profile has a phone number, and if not, send a friend request. When accepted see if their profile has any further information.

Remember the key is to get a method to speak with the lead. This is the best way to build rapport and have the opportunity for a long term relationship.

3. Insert in Database
Many Realtors make the mistake of waiting until they get ahold of the lead before adding them to a database. I recommend doing it at the first opportunity. You have paid money for every name and phone number you have. So protect that list. You never know when having something in your database will come in handy. Whether that is from someone calling years later after you gave up on them, or when you have a lull in your business and just need a

bunch of people to call. Every lead you buy should be kept so you can follow up with them in any of a number of ways.

4. Call Lead

Calling a lead does not mean picking up the phone and leaving a message or getting no answer. Calling a lead means to actually get ahold of the lead and speaking to someone. This means coming up with a plan to ensure that you are getting the most out of your leads. There will be leads we cannot get ahold of but we can't give up on the majority of leads solely because the first 1 or 2 calls don't end up with us talking to people.

The next thing you need to remember is it is not the leads job to call us back. It is our job to get ahold of the lead. Voicemail is not a Realtors friend, it lulls us into believing that we are doing something when we are not. Most leads especially internet leads will not call you back. So don't waste the time it takes to leave a voicemail unless you have a very good reason.

For each Realtor you need to come up with a game plan and system for your business. You need a standard which you will hold yourself to. I have already detailed the plans I have created for my business in the past in the chapter - Getting ahold of the Lead.

5. Quality Introduction

Ok so you call a lead and get ahold of someone. You now need a firm game plan of what to say. We have a chapter on using a quality script so I will not cover the reasons why again here.

The first step in the quality script you use is having a quick introduction which will answer the 2 basic questions all leads have the moment they answer the phone. "Who are you?" and "What do you want?"

You goal is to answer those quickly without bothering the lead. At this moment you are a Telemarketer. There is no way around that. So our job is to make the lead understand that they made us call them. I have included a full internet lead script in this book, and the introduction there does exactly what you need it to do.

TIP: - The next 4 million leads you talk to are "FINE" so you do not need to ask them how they are! This question is the most common mistake of any and all phone specialists. This question does not build rapport, it angers the person you are talking to. Get to answering their two questions and only if they ask you how you are should you ask them.

6. Gather Information
Once the telemarketer status is removed, you can head on to gathering some information about the lead. We want to determine their timing and motivation behind their real estate plans. However, as we discussed earlier these leads are very early in their process and often don't have solid information to share. It is here that old school scripting falls down on internet leads. Old school techniques are too direct and finite. The require the person you are talking to, to understand exactly what they want to accomplish.

For internet leads we need to be more cunning. Think of your leads as a deer in the woods and you are a hunter in a blind. Internet leads are deer that you can sort of see behind the trees and bushes. Old school techniques are about taking the shot, but at internet leads all you succeed in doing is scaring your target away. We need to use questions to control the conversation and gently coax information from the lead. One of the biggest keys to this is "The power of IF". If is a magical word that removes the finiteness of the leads situation. If allows them to provide a scenario and a possible outcome rather than 'make a promise' about what will happen. This difference will allow you to get so much more information from each lead you speak to and allow you to provide a higher level of service to your clientele.

The key to this step is to see what you can learn about the lead and determine a plan that includes your own personal belief as to when and why the lead will move.

Lastly when gathering information on Internet leads understand that they may not be looking to follow the correct and normal path just yet. If they have a home to sell, they may not be looking to get an evaluation or get it listed because they are still not sure that what they want is out there. Set yourself apart from the crowd by determining their desires and needs right now and following their path. Build rapport and trust then educate them to the plan they should follow when buying and selling. This will allow you a chance to meet with more people earlier in their process and building loyalty to you.

☐

7. Two outcomes

When you pick up a phone and dial an internet lead, we need to understand what is going to happen. Simply put only two things are going to happen at the end of the call. One, we are going to hang up and choose to never speak with the person on the other end of the phone again and two, we are going to have a plan of when we are going to speak with them again.

Obviously option one can be a very gratifying option at times, and can absolutely be the right choice too. However, I caution you agains choosing this option to freely. The result of choosing this option is both throwing away money already spent and the need to spend more money immediately. You need to have a standard in place for "why" we choose to never talk to the lead again. There are two main criteria that you need to use when building this standard.

1. Leads who treat me poorly. - They swear at me and will not follow any instruction, they "know more" than us experts and frankly deserve a life in exile from competent help.

Your competition will give up on them after the client is rude for the first time. Therefore to be different and better than them, you need to minimally move past this stage. After they are rude to me the second time, everyone else in Real Estate will give up on them, so to truly be the very best I need to allow them a Three Strike rule. This was always my mentality, and if I am being honest, many times I continued after this solely out of spite, just to cause them a little grief... and I ended up with booked appointments. So for me my straightforward answer is: Three Strikes and you're out.

2. Leads I talk to that are not doing anything soon. This will be the standard for internet leads. As we learned in the buyer cycle we will deal with more leads that are further out than we have in other lead generation systems. Do not lose perspective that we are creating a lifelong system of lead generation and client retention. So what is your standard of giving up on leads that are pleasant and friendly but they are over a year away from doing anything, or they say they will be doing something 'soon' every time you talk to them over a long period of time?

Your competition will give up on average after 3 conversations, the good agents, after 8 conversations, so to be the very best you can, never give up on this type of lead. They talk to you. Build rapport and minimally get referrals. In my opinion, they should never be given up on.

So there you have it, only when you are saying, I never want to speak to this person again, I never want to make money from this person, I would rather spend more money to get a new name and phone number than have to speak to this person again, only then should you choose option one.

Option two therefore becomes the standard. I need to make an offer of service and either book a face to face appointment or Book a Follow up call. There are 4 offers of service, a Buyer information Offer, Seller information Offer, Buyer Follow up offer and Seller Follow up offer. All the scripts I used are included in this book. These are simple to use Offer that provide immense value and appear to have no strings attached. Their job is to get the lead to agree that they want what we have.

8. Close for Appointment

The Close and the Offer are two separate steps. The Scripting has the closes that I recommend for internet lead conversion. The point here is that since your offer of service is about providing information which the client will agree to, we know they want the information we have. Then we need to tell them how to get that information. That is by meeting with us. We will know that when the client objects to us now it is solely the physical act of meeting that they are objecting to. This gives us vital information and allows us to be better prepared for them.

9. Handle Objections

First things first let me define the word objection for you so we are on the same page. Objections are <u>direct statements</u> from a client, customer or lead which are being used as an excuse not to do something with or get something from you the realtor. This 'something' could be signing a contract, making a legitimate offer, booking an appointment or simply obtaining information. People object to just about anything and everything at one time or another.

Now that we know what an objection is, let me take a moment to say what they are not. Objections are not legitimate reasons the person cannot do or get something. Sometimes objections and legitimate reasons look very similar so one needs to treat them the same until they know the excuse is real. How do you know the excuse is real? Well when you handle the excuse with quality and logic the objector continues with the same excuse. This means even though there is a logical solution it just will not solve their issue.

So what then is the best way to handle an objection? Well, it involves a Four step process. "LISA" – Listen, Identify, Solve and Ask.
- Step one   – Listen and Agree with The Person.
- Step two   – Identify and point out the problem with the persons thinking,
- Step three – Solve the person's problem.
- Step four   – Ask for closure.

I will go into more detail on each so that as you face objections in your future dealings you will know how to follow this approach.

Step one – Listen and agree with the person

This is a vital step in ensuring that you are handling the correct objection and creating an environment where the objector will listen to you as you continue to handle their problem. This is essential so we are not immediately perceived as arguing with the objector. We want to be viewed as someone who is on the same page as the Objector. We will accomplish nothing and not get the outcome we desire if we skip this step.

We will listen to what they are saying and identify the issue, possibly even clarify with a question to ensure we are on the same page. Remember the same objection can be said in a huge multitude of ways. Our next actions will be to agree with them in part. (Eg. "I'm Too Busy" – respond with, As a busy person yourself, you are well aware of ...) then continue on in the process. We do not argue that what they are saying is wrong, we agree with them (in part) even if they are wrong. We do this so that the person will listen to the remainder of the objection handle.

Step two – Identify and point out the problem with the persons thinking

Once we are seen as listing to them and agreeing with them we begin to turn the conversation to our agenda. We need to use the Objection to point out the flaw in the objector's issue. We need to show that the objection is actually part of the problem, not that which they are objecting too. (eg. ... the sheer volume of listings and information that is out there today and the time that it would take someone to navigate to the best information is truly daunting ...)

Step three – Solve the person's problem.

Now we need to show how what they are objecting to is the solution to the new problem we created together. We need to provide them a better way that when viewed logically will solve the clients issue and make the clients life easier and better. (eg. ...However what I am going to do will save you hours of time by making sure you are exposed to the very best information as quickly as possible....)

Step four – Ask for Closure.

This is easily the most skipped step in the process. Once we have identified the problem, showed the real issue and the solution to the problem, we must act confident as we now know the problem is solved. Using that confidence we must return to the original offer (of service, contracts, offer...) and ask again for what the client needs to do. (eg. ... it only takes 10-15 min now when is the best time for us to meet? {provide options of times i. E. Monday or Tuesday})

Conclusion

Now hopefully, since we have solved their "problem" they will now be closer to or in fact ready to book an appointment or write the offer, or do the action to which they were objecting to in the first place, once again if they repeat the same objection that is a sign that either we did a poor job providing the logical solution or the Objection is a Legitimate excuse.

It is also at this time where they might throw out a new objection. This is a sign they are still trying to avoid the necessary action we know is best for them. Handle this second objection using the same "LISA" technique. Provide a nice and firm approach and do your best to calm their worries. However, if they should come up with a third different objection, this is a sign that the client is being difficult and truly at this moment you are not going to be able to turn their mind without causing damage to your own reputation in their minds. At this point break off the conversation in a friendly way and let the client know you will revisit the subject in the future. Then go about your day, talk to more people and handle their objections, and more people and more objections.

Once you become a real wiz at this method you will be far more confident to talk to more people at anytime and in anyplace. You will see a marked improvement in your conversion skills which will in turn affect the bottom line. You will make more contacts with people because you know that you can handle anything they plan to throw at you. You know that if you don't help them know you can the next time you speak to them. You will frankly make more money and get more respect.

10. Book date and time, then location for the Appointment

I know this may seem like an easy step. But frankly there are somethings you can do here that can absolutely ruin your appointment. So lets walk through how to book the appointment with an internet lead. Remembering that they are a little more wary and hesitant to book than some other leads might be.

First when booking the appointment ask for 10-15 minutes of time, not 30 or 60. Everyone can find 10-15 minutes in his or her life; very few people can find a hour. The funny thing is most people will book 1 hour of time for that 10-15 min appointment any way. So always tell people it will take 10-15 minutes.

Next ask when it will work best for the lead, Days, evenings or weekends. Let them know their options and you will often get a better response. This is not old school cold calling where we need to say tuesday at 7 or 9 pm. Be more open and free, give the lead the feeling lie they are in charge, not that they are being bullied into an appointment.

Follow days, evenings weekends up by following the path the lead chooses. If they were to say days, respond with "What day this week works best for you?" Then "what time on Tuesday works best for you?". Until we have an appointment. The last optional step is to no provide the exact time they want. For instance if they say 6pm, I would respond wit "Oh I can't do 6, does 6:30pm work for you?" 99 times out of 100 it does. This is a subconscious message to the lead that they cannot always get what they want. It is a part of training your client how to behave. Now for the 1 time they can't move the appointment, then I say "OK I'm going to call my other appointment, I know they had some flexibility in the time they could meet and see if I can move it. If I can't move it, I will call you back, but for now lets say 6pm is Good and I will meet you."

At this point I will discuss location for the appointment. I am a firm believer in meeting in only 4 places;

1. The leads home,
2. My office,
3. The leads office,
4. A neutral site (I.e. Coffee shop).

Normally after the date and time are set, I will say, "Excellent, Do you know where my office is, or would you prefer that I came to your house?" I personally do not care between those two options and if there are issues will move on to the other two options. Frankly most of the time people will not care too much. "Oh I thought we could meet at the house" is simply an objection which is covered in the script book in this book.

Now the last step, which is frankly most often skipped is very important. After the date and time are finalized, and the location is agreed upon. finish booking the appointment by repeating — IN FULL — the date and time of the appointment. "Alright so we are meeting on Tuesday, October 1st at 6:30pm at your home, 123 Main St." The reason this is very important is because people remember commitments in two separate ways. Some are by the day of the week, "Suzie plays soccer on Wednesday nights." The other is by actual date. "I have a doctor's appointment on October 1st." By repeating the full date and time we make sure the lead can hear both styles and we can hopefully ensure that the appointment will not be cancelled because of an appointment they already have. Also by repeating the full date, we can catch holidays that otherwise would have escaped us like February 14th being Valentine's day.

11. Mortgage Broker Close
The actual script is attached in the script book, but this is the final phase of the call. After everything is booked and finalized, we want to introduce the concept of someone else calling the lead before our appointment. The point for us is to ensure financing is viable, but that is of very little benefit to the client. So this should be very quick and seem like an "afterthought". It should not let the lead know that it is a Mortgage Broker calling, but instead a team member. Over the years it has become very clear that the only think the public are more scared of than Sales people is Mortgage Brokers. The public views the Mortgage broker as the person who can make or break them. They are the person that will tell them what they are worth, and this can be a very scary thought. Because of that Mortgage Brokers have a hard time reaching the public. When you tell your lead a team member will be calling, then have that team member be a mortgage broker, the lead answers the phone 40% more than if you tell them a mortgage broker is calling. So do yourself, your clients and your mortgage broker a favour and tell people from now on that you are having a team member call them.

12. Reminder Call

If the appointment is booked more than 48 hours away, I strongly recommend making a reminder call before the appointment. The script is in this book. The real key to this is understanding that the reminder call is not simply a reminder of the date and time of the appointment. It is a reminder of the excitement and benefits of the appointment. What you need to know is that during the last call, you convinced the lead to actually meet with you. To go out of their comfort zone. Since that call their own brain as well as many of the people they spoke to have chipped away at their excitement about this appointment. They are strongly considering cancelling or not showing up at all. So when you call, you need to immediately reestablish that excitement and assure the lead they have made the right decision. Also this can be done on a physical call, over voicemail, by Text message or social media. You can use whatever source your lead will respond to best. Just make sure to choose your words properly and create that urgency and excitement for the appointment.

13. Book your Follow up.

Now all these steps have been about booking an appointment and sadly that is not the most common result of the calls you make. Most of the time you will not book an appointment. But that is OK. What we want to do is leave the call with the ability to make a follow up call in the future. To many people make a cardinal mistake here. Too many people ask "IF" they can follow up with the lead. To me this just sets up an awkward situation, for you see I am going to call approx. 95% of the leads back again. What I do is as the call is ending, I make a plan in my head of when I should call this lead back. In general that will be in 1-2 weeks, 1-2 months or 4-6 months. So I don't want them to say, no to me. Instead I always ask "WHEN" I should follow up. Sure some people will say "don't call me I'll call you" or some variation of that. To which I will reply "Great, Thanks and have a great day", I'll hang up and call them again in 3-4 months (or whenever appropriate). But most will do one of 3 things. 1. They will tell me to call back further away than I originally planned. Now a lead will not get me to change later. I trust myself more than I trust them. So if I was thinking 2 months and they say 1 year, I'll still call in 2 months. 2. They will tell me to call back on the same time frame as I was thinking. This is easy I just follow the plan I already had in my head. 3. Is they tell me something earlier than I was thinking. This is the important one, because this will change my plan completely and often ends up giving me further information that otherwise I would never have had. This third option doesn't happen all that frequently but when it does it is so important.

14. FOLLOW UP!

I have actually decided to put an entire portion of this book to follow up calls, frankly because they are just that important. I will simply say here, of all the fourteen steps, step 14 is both the most profitable step and the most ignored step in the entire chain. You can really change the future course of your business by improving your follow up skills, or in fact by actually doing follow up calls at all. For a more detailed and in-depth understanding of follow up calls head to "The Importance of Follow Up Calls".

Internet Lead Script

Hello is Jack there please? *(ask for person who requested information by first name)*

Speak Quickly

Hi Jack this is {salesperson} from {TEAM NAME} at {Company Name} I'm calling to let you know that we received <u>your request</u> for copies of {Homes for sale} in {Town Area} and I wanted to let you know that we are preparing that information and will be sending it to you. Is that ok?

Note: Do not ask, "How are you?" You only have a few seconds to get the client to understand that you are calling them back.

1. **Excellent, so, how long have you guys been thinking about making a move?**

2. **Great, If you did move, where do you hope to end up?**

3. **Wow, and when would you like to get this done if everything worked out perfectly?**

4. **That's exciting, Are you a first time buyer or do you have a house to sell?**

{Need to know what service the client is looking for}

B) if they have a house to sell ask:

Would you like to get out looking for your next home first or are you hoping to put your home on the market first?

5. **Do you have an agent in mind to help you when the time is right?**

B) IF THEY SAY YES ASK:

Are you 100% committed to that agent or are you open to hearing what different and better services I can offer to you?

NEXT ACTION: Make a Buyer Value Proposition/ Make a Seller Value Proposition / Make a Follow-up Offer / or Say Goodbye

Buyer Offer

This is the standard offer for anyone looking to buy a home for any reason. It is very hard to say no to. Not until the client says yes to this offer do we move on to close for an appointment. Note without an appointment we do not do anything in the buyer offer for a lead. This offer is for any "Buy first", "Look first" or "First time buyer clients" we talk to.

Buyer Offer

Well, what I can do for you is get you daily access to all the information on the homes that match what you're looking for. You will have the address, price and all available photos, all the information just like a Realtor gets. It will update you instantly by sending out only what is NEW or had a price change, to ensure you have the best information. Oh, and our clients also have gain access to bank sales, estate sales and other distress sales, would you be interested in those great deals as well?

{This extra information can be anything you choose that is of great interest to the client i.e. for investors- a list of the top 10 investment deals each week...}

Appointment Setting:

Excellent, what we need to do next is meet for about 10-15 min to take down your exact wants and needs. **When is the best time to do this - DAYS EVENINGS OR WEEKENDS?**

Note: We do not ask for permission to meet. Deal with the objections as they come.

Once you have the appointment Date and Time worked out:

Ok, so our appointment is (full date and time e.g. "Tuesday, October 1st at 6pm with {agent's name}").

a. a)   Would you like to come into our office or have our agent (Me) come out to your home?

b. b)   Do you know where our office is? (if you want appointment at the office only)

c. c)   I have your address as {123 Primrose} is that correct? (if the have a home to sell)

They respond - Then:

After we set you up for the e-mails, would you like (the agent, "Me", "John" etc...) to give you a rough idea on the value of your home in today's market?

Note: we want to say the full date to jog any memory of another appointments or obstacles that they might have forgotten about.

Finish with:

Excellent, what is going to happen next is one of our Team Members will give you a call before the appointment. They are going to ask you a few questions so that we can be more prepared for our meeting and ensure we provide you with a quality set of listings to kick start your home search. Also If you would like to know a little more about us, visit (www.socialproofsite.com) Other than that we will see you on {appointment date} Thank you.

NEXT ACTION: Enter notes in your CRM

Seller Offer

Here are the offers you can make to a selling client, There are less objections because sellers know they need to meet with an agent to list their home.

Seller Offer

Well, what I can do for you is give you a Full Marketplace Evaluation on your house in today's market. We can also discuss what the right time to put your home up for sale is and the costs that are involved so you know exactly what to expect. Oh and my clients also get access to some tips and tricks that on average increase the value of your home by about 5%. Would you be interested in that as well?

The Close (Cost):

All we need to do now is book at time for us to come over, when is the best time for you, DAYS, EVENINGS OR WEEKENDS.

BOOK DATE and TIME and AGENT

Excellent, what is going to happen next is one of our Team Members will give you a call before the appointment. They are going to ask you a few questions so that we can be more prepared for our meeting and ensure we provide you with a quality set of listings to kick start your home search. Also If you would like to know a little more about us, visit (www.socialproofsite.com) Other than that we will see you on {appointment date} Thank you.

Buyer Objections

These Objection handles need to be posted anywhere you handle calls. The Key to handling any objection is to solve their objection with a Benefit to them. Make them comfortable and they will meet.

I don't have time to meet:

You know this as made for a busy person like you. Sending all the information to your e-mail makes it so you can check it whenever you want. Plus it will save you time simply because you will have full access to the information about the homes that interest you. It takes 10-15 min now but will save you hours and hours during the process of looking for your next home; what is better for you Days, Evenings or Weekends?

I need to check with my spouse:

Well, that's a great idea, let's set a tentative time that normally works for you and your spouse a few days from now, then you can speak with them and I'll give you a call the day before to confirm that it still works for the both of you; no one will show up without us speaking again, so what usually works best for your spouse, Days, Evenings or Weekends?

<u>Just send me the emails, I can tell you right now what I want:</u>

I know that you have a firm understanding of what you are looking for in your next home, and in order to do a good job for you, I need to be on that same page. I'm going to sit down and take the proper time to get a firm grasp of what you want, this way I don't waste your time by sending out hundreds of homes that don't match what you are looking for or worse than that, missing out on that <u>great</u> deal, it only takes 10-15 min and then we are on our way to finding you your next home; what is better for you Days, Evenings or Weekends?

<u>I'm already getting that info online:</u>

The internet is a great place to start your home search. The problem is that it is usually behind often by weeks or months, and as I'm sure you are aware, the good deals go quickly! What I'm offering to you now is far superior, I will get you access to all the real estate information just like a realtor gets. What you are going to receive will update you daily what is new on the market or had a price change, so you are one of the first people to know about the great deals. It only takes 10-15 min and then we are on our way to finding you your next home; what is better for you Days, Evenings or Weekends?

<u>(Point 2Agent.com / you / your site) set me up already for the emails: (if you have a service like this)</u>

That's a great place to start, what you have signed up for includes my listings and those that others have allowed me to send. What I'm offering to you now is far superior, I will get you access to all the real estate information just like I get as a realtor. What you are going to receive will update you daily what is new on the market or had a price change, so you are one of the first people to know about the great deals. It only takes 10-15 min and then we are on our way to finding you your next home; what is better for you Days, Evenings or Weekends?

<u>I'm not going to sign anything!</u>

I understand. *You* don't have to sign a thing. We are just going to get you the information you need to make a quality Real Estate decision.

Seller Objections

What Commission do you charge? (Most popular Objection)
Well, with us, you are in control of that, we have a few service packages available ranging from 3.5% to 7% commission. We will explain them all to you and you will choose which service you would like. When is the best time for us to come over, Days, Evenings or Weekends?

I can't book without talking to my spouse/ other:
Well, that's a great idea, let's set a tentative time that normally works for you and your spouse a few days from now, then you can speak with them and I'll give you a call the day before to confirm that it still works for the both of you; no one will show up without us speaking again, so what usually works best for your spouse, Days, Evenings or Weekends?

Can you send me an evaluation by email?
I can send you an email with a rough idea on value. However, in order to do an accurate job for you, we need to see your home. As I'm sure you are aware, the inside of your home affects the value a great deal. It only takes about 30 minutes and we also give you those tips that on average improve the value of your home by about 5%; what's better for you, Days, Evenings or Weekends?

I already know the value of my home:

That's great, would you also like to learn some low-cost ways to raise the value of your home by about 5%? Also we can show you some innovative techniques to get your home sold for the most amount of money in the least amount of time. Would you be interested in that information as well?

I don't know when I'll be available. / I don't have any time. / I'm simply too busy right now to meet:

I understand everyone is very busy these days, this is why we work 9am to 10pm, 7 days a week. We take less than an hour and it is a Free of charge, no obligation Evaluation. Once this is done, we will do everything else, what time would it be best for us to come by?

Mortgage Broker Close

Excellent, what is going to happen next is one of our Team Members will give you a call before the appointment. They are going to ask you a few questions so that we can be more prepared for our meeting and ensure we provide you with a quality set of listings to kick start your home search. Also If you would like to know a little more about us, visit (www.socialproofsite.com) Other than that we will see you on {appointment date} Thank you.

For First Time buyers – have a mortgage broker do this call, all others, this call can be done by any Team Member or a mortgage Broker if you wish, point is to qualify the appointment in terms of financing and motivation

Reminder Call

Now that we have booked an appointment, the next big challenge is actually getting the client to show up. To help improve the percentages, use a Reminder call. A call that does not simply CONFIRM the appointment date and time, but reminds the client of the benefits and the reasons they booked the appointment in the first place.

Knowing this we need a script to remind the client about what we are doing at the appointment, reinvigorate their excitement level and remind them when and where the appointment is. We need to try a couple of times to speak to the Client on the phone, however, this is one time where leaving a message is ok as well.

It needs to be done the night before the appointment or the morning of the appointment at the very latest.

Like in anything this is not a foolproof solution but will increase your face to face appointments.

Reminder Call: Voice mail

Hi {name} this is (agent) calling from (company or Team/Company). I wanted to let you know that I've gotten some great things organized for our appointment. I know you are going to be excited by what is available for you right now. So we are meeting tomorrow at (TIME) at (LOCATION) and I can't wait to meet you and get you this great information.

Plus I know you will be really happy receiving the daily updates which include Estate Sales, power of sales and other distressed properties. This way you will never miss out on a great deal.

Ok, as you can tell, I am really excited about helping you find a great deal on your next home. I look forward to seeing you tomorrow.

If you need to reach me, my cell number is ...

This can be used as a Voice mail as well, but attempt to reach the client at least twice before leaving the message.

CHAPTER SEVEN
Realistic Expectations

"Most of us spend too much time on what is urgent and not enough time on what is important."
~~Stephen R. Covey

As you become a phone specialist or have added one to your team, it becomes increasingly obvious that there needs to be goals and expectations put on the role. We have already talked about "when to give up on a lead' which is a common worry, but throughout this chapter, I want to discuss what the phone specialist's day should look like and how to know what has occurred during that day.

When should I call?

Weekday:

8:30am-11:00am: — are the best morning hours to call, however you run the risk of bothering people as they are getting ready for the day. It is also a good time for people with work phone numbers as often people are looking for a way to procrastinate before starting at work.

11:00am – Noon: This is a difficult hour to reach people, if at work they are trying to get some work done before lunch so the morning has not been a complete waste, or so they can get out for lunch.

Noon-3:00pm: A time to call people are on their lunch break or just returned to work and looking for a distraction before starting to work again.

3:00-5:00pm: – is the WORST time to try and speak to people – if at work they are now getting on task to get things complete before they have to go home, if at home, the kids are returning from school and they are trying to deal with them.

5:00-7:00pm: – This is a tough time and you will get "dinnertime" calls, where you will speak to people but they will have a higher level of frustration because they are driving home or sitting at the dinner table.

7:00-8:00pm: – A great hour to call, some left over dinner time people but in general more relaxed and ready to discuss other thoughts in their lives such as real estate.

8:00-9:30pm: – Single best time to call during the week. 8 to 9 is normal and when you are on a roll throwing in the extra 30 min is well worth it. Any later and you are bothering people who are in bed. This 1 hour or 1:30min of calling is worth 2-3 hours at any other time of the day.

Weekend and Stat holidays:

Saturday:
9:00-12:00 – this is the best time to get a hold of people these hours are equal to the 8:00-9:00pm time slot during the weekday.

12-9pm – As long as people are still answering the phone, dial! The nicer the weather the tougher the afternoons and evenings become.

Sunday:
The rules for Sundays depend on your area. If you are in a heavily religious area, calling on Sundays can offend some people. In fact depending on the religion in the area

this "offensive period" could happen at other times of the week as well. Know your area don't call when people will be offended. Other than this, Sundays are the same as Saturdays except I would start a little later in the day as many people like to sleep in on Sundays.

Stat Holidays:
These can be the best days of the year to reach people, and typically they are is a great mood. Obviously the more 'religious' the day the more angry people are with 'telemarketers' of any type. That said some of my very best days were during Stat holidays. I strongly recommend coming in and calling on those days.

How long on any given day?
In general a Phone specialist should look at doing six 6 hour shifts every week. Mostly nights and weekends with some daytime calling to ensure we are trying to reach people we can't get ahold of throughout the entire day. (3-9pm, 9am-3pm shifts) You should take at least two 15 min breaks and one 30min break for a meal.

How many leads?
A quality phone specialist needs 150-200 leads a month to turn around the results we are looking for. However each month this number should fluctuate depending on the size of the follow up business in their database. The phone specialist should have 300 plus names to dial any given day. An Active agent would require between 30-50 new leads a month if there is no Phone Specialist help available. Beyond this number and the Active agent will make a sufficient living from dealing with only the very best leads, and will discard any lead that needs follow up or future effort.

How often to call a new lead before giving up?

The following is the requirements I made on my phone specialist staff in the past to get a hold of a lead.

When given a new lead the phone specialist will make three attempts a day for seven days. For clarification that is days of calling so if they work a six-day shift it should take approximately 8 days to accomplish this (21 calls). Then once a day for the next 7 days (total 28 dials), at this point they can leave a voice mail. Then they should put the lead off to dial seven days in the future. Then they should dial it once a day for fourteen more days (total 42 dials), and then if they want they could give up on that lead as unreachable. This provides a level of expectation that no Active Agent could ever accomplish. Only a phone specialist can do this, and it allows the specialist the ability to "suck the marrow from the bones" and allows the team to get more out of the current marketing budget.

If we speak to the lead, in general I would rarely give up ever. To reiterate the key point made in the "When to give up on a lead" chapter, even those people being rude to me will speak to me one or two more times. I simply need to speak to them when they need me and my services and they will cease to be rude, and book an appointment.

Dry spells happen!
This is an inevitability of the phone specialist, a period of time where nothing seems to go right. No one is meeting with you, the no show rate is through the roof and our own mentality begins to fade. This is the true test of a phone specialist.

How to over come these dry spells.
The first and most important thing to do is CONTINUE DIALING. It is also the hardest thing to do. The lower the results go, the lower our drive to dial the phone. Remember that when things are going bad, your 'dial

'numbers should be higher. You need to push through the pain.

Next you need to be self-evaluating. After each call replay the call and determine if you like what you were saying. Use your script book here and be overly critical of your own work. Get back to basics and use the scripts word for word. Becoming complacent in scripting is the leading cause for most dry spells. Read your scripts a few times before calling and truly prepare yourself just as you did in the beginning.

Get the right attitude, even if it is fake. I am a big believer in mantra's and affirmations. Say to yourself that you love the job, love to dial and are about to book an appointment before every call. Force a smile on your face, and force positive energy out your mouth when you speak. Be excited about helping people again. It all seems a bit silly but works wonders time and time again.

Lastly know that you are not alone, dry spells happen to all of us and the best news is that the flip side is about to come, your "Midas days', you know the man with the golden touch, where everything will go right and those are the days we all live for.

"My experience has shown me that the people who are exceptionally good in business aren't so because of what they know, but because of their insatiable need to know more." ~~ Milton Hershey

This is the toughest simple thing to do. It is true, it has a feeling of big brother is watching, but without the right tracking nothing else that a phone specialist does is worth it's salt. This is the tool that allows you to know your results and in doing so allows you to look for ways to improve things, and project what the future will hold. Without it you are just dialing a phone and hoping it will all work out. With it you are able to predict results and determine how much you want to make each year and accomplish it.

Tracking is very simple; I believe it is still best accomplished with pen and paper on a simple form on a daily basis. This paper form may then be compiled into an electronic mass tracking system, but that should be done by someone more suited to that task than a salesperson or a phone specialist. The form must be completed daily but could be built to accommodate a weeks worth of information and therefore handed in once a week.

For tracking purposes we need to know what to look at and what should be expected on a day in and day out basis. A minimal amount of tracking would entail "Tracking your TACO". This would be your Talked to, Appointments booked, Contracts Signed and Offers. However as you become busier and larger you will Track more then just those items. Attempts, Talked to, Buyer Interviews, Appointments, Messages left, Call Backs (from messages), Follow up calls booked, cancellations, no shows and DEAD Leads. I will discuss what you should expect from the most important categories as your phone specialist becomes more and more effective. However, first I will define the terms I use to ensure you and I have the same understanding regarding my terms.

Attempts:
This is a generic term and refers to the number of times the phone is picked up in an attempt to speak with someone regarding real estate. So this would be an outgoing dial, whether the person answered the phone or not and incoming calls that you answered looking to talk to someone. One can also (an should also) have more than one dial per day for any specific person. This is not looking to determine how many people did I try to reach but how many attempts did I make to try and reach someone.

Talked To:
This is a generic term referring to the number of people I spoke to "about Real Estate" with the ability to book an appointment during the tracking period. If I call a number and speak to the wrong person this is not a contact. If I answer a phone looking for a lead and speak with an agent inquiring on behalf of his client, this is not a contact, but both examples would be a dial.

Buyer Interview:

This is a generic term for a face-to-face meeting where the ultimate goal should be to book an Appointment. (eg. – a showing, an Open house meeting) This is a new way to look at these huge time wasters in Real Estate. The most successful agents and teams have eliminated this from their tasks.

Appointment:

This is a generic term referring to a face-to-face meeting with a client with the ultimate goal and ability to sign a contract for services, specifically a Buyer Representation Agreement or a Listing agreement. NOTE: a showing without a meeting before or after is not an appointment.

Cancellations:

When a lead cancels a previously booked appointment before the appointments scheduled time. This may occur by telephone, email or even during a Reminder call. If an appointments date and time are simply changed that is not a cancellation, however if the client cancels then we later rebook the appointment it will count as a cancellation and a new appointments for statistical purposes.

No Show:

When a client does not show up for a previously scheduled appointment without informing the agent beforehand. This is a part of the Real Estate business and any Phone Specialist worth their salt has a no show rate, the goal is to keep it as low as possible. Often this is a sign of booking a lead for an appointment too soon or pushing certain personality types to hard for a face-to-face appointment.

Messages Left: A voice mail is left for a lead. For me this is a major waste of time and should be used VERY sparsely. If a message is left I recommend the following script. "Hi {Client first name} it's {first name} call me back at {Number}."

Call backs: Directly from the voice mail message left

Follow up Calls booked – A lead is spoken to, and we determine a time in the future when we should call again to check up on the status of their plans.

DEAD leads: A lead I no longer wish to contact ever again. Examples – Wrong number, already bought and sold, excessively rude. These leads should be forwarded to the team leader (they should also be few and far between).

Now we are on the same page about what the terms mean, lets look at what an effective completed tracking sheet should look like.

A phone specialist with a quality work ethic and the leads to dial should be making 160-220 dials a day based on a 6 hour shift. They should have talked to 30-50 people a day. They should be expected to book 2 appointments per calendar day ... a month with 30 days = 60 appointments, regardless of the number of days they work (unless of course they go away on vacation). Cancelations are a part of business and should be kept under 15%, while no shows will fluctuate depending on the expertise of the specialist, and the stage of the leads in the buying cycle. A phone specialist who is using mainly Internet and stealth advertising leads can expect a no show rate in the 20-40% range fluctuating month to month.

These numbers will give you a guideline to know if the phone specialist is working hard enough and smart enough. Some people will exceed these numbers and some will fall short, you need to pick the "important ones" to you and make sure they are being met. Tracking can be used to emphasize a point as well, such as the waste of time leaving messages is. As the Phone specialist proves themselves the need for exact number of dials is relaxed, accept a rough estimate of dials. This is usually 2-3 months into the phone specialist's tenure. At this point I will also start tracking Appointments Met, and No Show Appointments, while removing the Messages left and Call Backs from Messages.

At the end of the day this tracking will allow you to forecast earnings for the phone specialist as well as the team. It will allow you to know the cost effectiveness of what you are doing and make budgeting a far easier task. Without it, you are flying blind and just hoping that things will work out.

CHAPTER EIGHT
The Importance of Follow-up Calls

> "The three great essentials to achieve anything worthwhile are, first, hard work; second, stick-to-itiveness; third, common sense."
> ~~ Thomas Edison

This is a simple topic but one that 99.9% of all Real Estate people fail to do from time to time. It is the true turning point in each and every Real Estate business out there. The quality and consistency of follow up skills and follow up time spent is directly linked to the cost effectiveness in our marketing.

Whenever I speak on this topic I lead into it as a topic that will allow us to make more money without spending any more dollars. It is truly this important in each and every one of our businesses. Now I am not the first to write about the power of follow up, nor will I be the last, but for Real Estate I wanted to specifically target who and how often we should be doing follow up. Specifically the PHONE follow up - I personally never believe that Email or Mailers count as a contact.

Whenever we create an abundance of leads, we will end up being able to put those leads into two categories. Those we spoke to, and those we didn't. For those we spoke to we have four additional categories;

- Those we booked an appointment with
- Those doing something in near future
- Those doing something in the far future
- Those who were rude to us

This is a total of 5 groups of people and the very best organizations in the world have a Follow up protocol for each group.

One simple thing anyone can implement is the final question to ask any lead who is not booking an appointment. The direct quote, "I love to keep in touch with my clients, when would be a good time for me to follow up with you?" is a great tool to help determine which group the lead falls into. Please not I'm not asking IF I can follow up, but When I should. They will give me a time frame, and sometimes it will be very different from what I was thinking. This time frame allows me to place them in the correct category. Once we know what category they belong in, we can determine our protocol. Each organization needs to build their own, and there is no perfect system, but I will give my thoughts on each group and how often they should be followed up with.

Booked Appointment:
Obviously for those that booked an appointment with us, we hope that the appointment was good and the client signed with us and at that point other protocol takes over. But what about the appointments where they didn't sign with us? When should we call them back, how often and what should we say. This is the most over looked group with the most potential up side amongst the follow up calls.

Real Estate people tend to give up after meeting with people if they do not get what they want. Each lead should have a follow up plan built after the appointment with weekly to monthly calls as needed. I would also add a hand written note to be dropped off at their home within 48 hours. Some emails can be used, but not as a replacement for calling.

Near Future:
For the leads with near future business we need to have a plan with ever other week to monthly calls and rapport building techniques. This is the group where most follow up is currently done. However most organizations do not contact them frequently enough. Nor do they provide some free information or other "(free) gifts" to help build rapport. As well as an Email Drip campaign targeted to them.

Long Term Future:
For the leads in the far future, these should be contacted two to four times a year, the calls should be friendly and not pushy, they should leave the lead with a good positive feeling about dealing with you in the future. This doesn't mean we are not trying to set appointments, but many of these appointments will be in the future not today. This is a very often overlooked category where the future of our business lies while we cannot be caught up spending hours and hours of time here, a little effort can go a long way with this group of people. Their own Email drip "touch" campaign here works in conjunction with the calling.

Rude and Not Talked to:
Now the last two groups in my mind should be treated the same, and we can add in any other leads we have given up on for any reason. These leads need to be placed in a big batch and contacted in two different situations.

First whenever a new person joins the organization, their first few weeks on the phones should be dealing with the leads that no one has gotten ahold of or that were rude to us in the past or that we have given up on over time. These calls are for training purposes, and appointments are gravy, and in fact every time I have seen this done, appointments are booked from this group of "misfit leads".

The other situation is whenever we are having a lull in business or a lull in lead production. This group of leads always seems to produce, time changes people and it is amazing what an impact on our business these leads can have.

Something to think about is the fact that 66% of the appointments that are available in the leads we create are available **only** through follow up. Yet most organizations are extremely lacking in follow up systems. This category truly is the greatest place that we can make changes to see huge results in the bottom line without any huge investment of dollars. It is the first place that every organization should look to improve their skills and the most cost effective way to improve our bottom line.

Follow-up Offers
Buyer Follow-up Offer
When you have done all you can for the lead for now but you want to speak to them again, set up a follow-up call.

Well (Name) we love to keep in touch with our clients, when do think would be the best time for me to follow up with you? *(Don't ask can I call you back, just ask when!)*

Excellent, also if you want to know a little more about us please visit (<u>www.socialproofsite.com</u>). Thank you for your time today. Good bye.

Seller Follow-up
This is used to set up a follow up call with a lead that is not ready to list their home and is not interested in any Buyer information.

What I can do for you is send you a quick email with everything that has been listed or sold in your area in the last little while. It will include the addresses, pictures and price so you can compare them to your home. This will give you a rough idea of what your home is worth in today's market. Then when you are closer to listing we will come out and give you a much more accurate evaluation at that time. How does that sound?

Well (Name) we love to keep in touch with our clients, when do think would be the best time for me to follow up with you?

Excellent, also if you want to know a little more about us please visit (<u>www.socialproofsite.com</u>). Thank you for your time today. Good bye.

CHAPTER NINE

Setting up your Workspace

Setting up your office

The Studio, a room to which the artist consigns himself for life, is naturally important, not only as a workplace, but as a source of inspiration. ~~~ Grace Glueck

This may seem a bit strange, but there are a whole slew of benefits that can come from having a well set up workplace. It will allow you to become more fluent on the phone in any and all situations.

Personally I find windows to be overrated, but for many people they are a necessity, you will need to know what is better for yourself. However, I believe nice pictures or paintings can provide just as much scenery with far less distraction.

For the Aesthetic minded of us out there, I believe painting an office in a pleasing colour provides for better longer lasting energy. The stark white or off white workplaces that I regularly see are not conducive to a calm and relaxed phone specialist. Personally I like rich beiges, greens and blues. But I would choose a colour the actual person working in the office likes. This may seem like a silly expense to paint, but the fresh environment will pay you back for sure.

Famous quotes and pictures of goals are important. Quotes that are the persons favourite, or ones that reflex what the team is striving to accomplish. Not all quotes should be "work harder" quotes, some should be funny, and uplifting quotes others can be focus and driven based quotes. These can be fancy posters or simply print outs on paper. Pictures of Goals are personal and should be chosen and placed by the phone specialist.

Tracking needs to have a central location and be always present while not over powering the room. It should not be placed where the specialist must look at it all the time, but be handy for when they need to see it. It should include a tally board with Appointments booked, Appointments Met, No Shows and Contracts signed for each agent who is having appointments booked for them. This should be out in the open for all to see. There should be a monthly calendar used as an Appointments booked per day tally board. All phone specialists should be putting the number of appointments booked on a day on the same calendar. Lastly and this should be the smallest board, there should be a Deal Tracker for transactions completed that the specialists booked the original appointment.

Most important is the personal workspace for the Phone specialist. They need a desk, phone, headset, pens and paper and a computer. They should have their own space that they use every time they call. Some of the essentials in setting up this space is a Large Print version of the Script book, which should be taped to the wall all around the phone. They can be in any order that the specialist deems appropriate, but for me I had my phone in a central location on the desk just to the right of my computer. Right above it on the wall was my Buyer Offer, and above that the seller offer and at the top of that the introduction script with my 'five questions'. To the left I had my buyer objections, to the right was first a Mirror, then the Seller Objections, all objections were in order from most common to least common.

This allowed me to at the drop of a hat look on my wall and ensure that I would be word for word perfect when delivering my scripts, even if I forgot a part or stumbled. Truthfully I rarely used the scripts up there during a call, but they were instrumental in my post call evaluation, and were a saviour now and then when I would have a brain fart.

The mirror was a good tool for reminding me about posture, smiling and my energy level. It helps to centre you and ensure the proper attitude while dialing the phone.

Lastly I only mentioned in passing the headset, I believe 100% that a headset is an imperative tool for the phone specialist. It reduces fatigue, and allows the freedom of movement for note taking and using a computer. Not providing a headset will reduce the phone specialists dial rate by 33-45%, which far outweighs any costs attached to this piece of equipment. Personally I have used both Corded and wireless headsets. Wireless allows for much more freedom, even if there is a long cord on the corded one. That said if costs are an issue, the main benefits lie in the headset itself not its cord or lack there of.

CHAPTER TEN
Bonus

It's just madness. First email. Then instant message. Then MySpace. Then Facebook. Then LinkedIn. Then Twitter. It's not enough anymore to 'Just do it.' Now we have to tell everyone we are doing it, when we are doing it, where we are doing it and why we are doing it.
~~~Mark McKinnon

Leads are now also coming in the form of text messages. Either from signs, print ads or the internet. These leads again need to have a new approach. They are absolutely great because a text message will give you a valid cell phone number which people are less likely to avoid answering. But they still need to be treated with kid gloves like internet leads.

They are not yet ready to deal with a Real Estate agent, so you need to be calm, be an information provider and council them as to the right choice on how to proceed. The Introduction to the call is a bit different and I have included it here. We are really trying to determine if the text lead is an Ad/Sign call or more like an internet lead (Where are they in the buyer cycle?). Once you know that, you follow that path to the possible appointment.

Instant Text Leads

Hello this is _____ from_____ at _____, we saw that you sent us a text about one of our listings and I am calling to make sure the system worked properly and sent the correct information out to you, did you receive the information you requested?

Did the information you received answer all of your questions?

If No:

What information were you looking for? (DON"T ANSWER _LOOK UP THE ANSWERS and continue on the SIGN/AD CALL SCRIPT)

If Yes:

Excellent because we love to help out our clients anyway we can, so let me ask you;

(HEAD TO THE INTERNET LEAD SCRIPT)

How to learn a Script

"Practice is where you BECOME the very best in the world, Game day is when you prove it."
~~ Andy Herrington

Learning a script WORD for WORD is a major struggle for many people. I wish I could say that there is one simple way to do it, however there just isn't. It is a very personal thing. I will however give you a bunch of different ideas on how to tackle scripting and learn it as best you can.

The biggest key to any of these ideas is repetition. Doing it over and over again until it is ingrained in your brain. The idea is to get to the point where the words are simply a part of you and you do not need to think at all as they flow out from you.

Ways to Learn a Script:

Mental Repetition: this is where you read the words over and over in your mind. You think the words and test yourself by removing the visual words. This is one of the most commonly used and most difficult ways to learn a script; I honestly do not recommend it at all.

Vocal Repetition: This is where you read the words out loud over and over. You speak the words and test yourself by removing the visual words. The most common mistake in this format is trying to learn the entire piece at once, rather than breaking it up sentence-by-sentence and learning each sentence by itself. Imagine a paragraph with 4 sentences. The best way to use Vocal repetition is to say only sentence 1 over and over again until you can do it without the paper in hand. Then move to sentence 2 and learn it the same then combine sentence 1 & 2... This is a very good way to learn a script.

Written Repetition: For many people writing out the script over and over, first copying word for word from another piece of paper then from memory, and checking it against a good copy. The step of checking it tends to be missed which has the side effect of ingraining mistakes instead of correcting them. This is usually a great tool as an add on to another technique, but for certain people can work well all on its own.

Pneumatic Devices: Just like in grade school, BEDMAS for math, or ROYGBIV for the colours of the rainbow, pneumatic devices can help you out. They can be exactly like that remembering things in the right order by letters putting things into a 'sing-song' format, or more likely for adults by using actions. The brain is amazing, if you say the same thing over and over and associate it with an action, like touching your thumb and index finger, the two will become linked. This means that you can then touch your thumb and index finger together and that action will help you remember the words to say. Don't believe me, try it you will be amazed.

Role Play: Practicing real life scenarios with another person is by far the best way to learn a script. The competition aspect if you are both learning is also helpful. However make sure you have someone there that is listening for and being critical of the mistakes.

Self – Evaluation: As you role play, or even get on the phones, self-evaluation is a major key in learning your scripts and keeping your scripts accurate over time. Take a moment after any role play, call or practice session and evaluate what you did right and wrong. What you need to focus on improving and what you used to do and no longer are doing. This time is where you truly improve.

Lastly I want to give you an idea on how long it takes to learn a script. For most people who are working at it everyday, and spending time incorporating numerous tactics to learn the script, it should take 2-4 weeks to be able to comfortably say the script from memory. However, It will then take 2-4 months to ingrain that script into your brain so you do not have to think about what you are saying as you say it. This is where you have achieved true WORD for WORD knowledge of the script. So give yourself enough time to learn the script and use it.

Andy Herrington

About the Author

Andy Herrington is a Canadian Real Estate Salesperson, International Author, High Energy Speaker and Real Estate Business Coach. He was a part of 3 of the Top Real Estate Sales Teams on Canada's Largest Real Estate Board. For 6 Years, he was an active member and manager for the different team's Inside Sales Teams as a bonifide Phone Specialist. During this stretch these teams averaged over 350 sales a year, and completed in excess of 2100 deals. In 4 of those 6 years the team he was on ranked #1 on Canada's Largest Real estate Board, the Toronto Real Estate Board for Units sold or Volume of sales.

Andy went on to be the Director of Coaching and a Master Coach for the first "Team Specific" training company Dan Plowman Team Systems. He stayed there for 4 years, before branching off on his own to develop and build Powerhouse Coaching Inc. This allowed Andy the freedom to use all of the knowledge from all of the teams he has been a part of either as Team Member or as a Master Coach.

Over the years Andy has coached 7 of the Top 15 Producers in the Toronto Real Estate Board, as well as the Top Producer in 5 other Canadian Real Estate Boards. Andy has helped Real Estate Salespeople all across Canada strive to do better and make the Industry a more professional place.

Andy has had numerous articles published internationally as well as in Canada, most notably in SOLD Magazine and REM magazine. He runs a blog @ andyherrington.com and can be seen at speaking engagements across North America. You can find out more information about his coaching program @ www.powerhousecoaching.ca and you can buy his other books @ www.powerhousedialing.com.

Lastly to inquire about having Andy speak to your team or brokerage or have Andy as your coach, or your teams coach contact him directly @ andy@andyherrington.com, you will not be disappointed.

40296713R00080

Made in the USA
Charleston, SC
03 April 2015